face2face

Advanced Workbook

Nicholas Tims
with Gillie Cunningham & Jan Bell

CAMBRIDGE
UNIVERSITY PRESS

CAMBRIDGE UNIVERSITY PRESS
Cambridge, New York, Melbourne, Madrid, Cape Town, Singapore,
São Paulo, Delhi, Dubai, Tokyo

Cambridge University Press
The Edinburgh Building, Cambridge CB2 8RU, UK

www.cambridge.org
Information on this title: www.cambridge.org/9780521712798

First published 2009
Reprinted 2010

Printed in Dubai by Oriental Press

A catalogue record for this publication is available from the British Library

ISBN 978-0-521-71279-8 Workbook with Key
ISBN 978-0-521-71278-1 Student's Book with CD-ROM
ISBN 978-0-521-71280-4 Teacher's Book
ISBN 978-0-521-71281-1 Class Audio Cassettes (3)
ISBN 978-0-521-71282-8 Class Audio CDs (3)
ISBN 978-0-521-74047-0 Classware CD-ROM (single classroom)
ISBN 978-0-521-74581-9 Test Generator CD-ROM

Contents

1 Let's talk

1A Make a good impression

Communicating V1.1

 Read what Martin, Ros, Maggie and Nigel say about communication at work. Choose the correct word/phrase for each gap.

Martin

I'm a talkative person. I know that. I love ¹ _b)_ and the first thing I do when I get to work is have a ² .... with the people who sit around me. I suppose people could accuse me of just ³ .... about stuff – last night's TV, the price of food and so on. For me, it just makes the day go more quickly.

Ros

People think I'm arrogant at times. I tend to ⁴ .... when I'm in meetings and that can annoy people. But sometimes I do it with the best of intentions. As a lawyer, I ⁵ .... with people who are in stressful situations. If two people are about to ⁶ .... , it's better to stop the situation before it goes too far.

Maggie

I'm uncharacteristically quiet at work because I'm in an open-plan office – there are no walls. So I tend to ⁷ .... a lot of people's conversations. The guy who sits next to me is constantly ⁸ .... with his girlfriend on the phone. It can be terribly embarrassing. And then five minutes later, he starts a friendly conversation with me – almost ⁹ .... It's awful!

Nigel

Most people think I'm quite shy but I just don't talk that much. ¹⁰ .... about the love lives of famous people, or who is or isn't getting on with who, isn't my thing. One thing I hate is people who ¹¹ .... One of my colleagues spends all day moaning about how much work she's got to do. I spend most of my time trying to avoid ¹² .... with her in case she thinks I'm interested.

1	a) bickering	(b)) chatting	c) rowing
2	a) talk	b) row	c) chat
3	a) wittering on	b) butting in	c) overhearing
4	a) butt in	b) witter on	c) chat up
5	a) get in touch	b) make eye contact	c) come into contact
6	a) have a row	b) bicker	c) grumble
7	a) gossip about	b) overhear	c) come into contact with
8	a) bickering	b) gossiping	c) wittering on
9	a) having a row	b) chatting	c) chatting me up
10	a) Chatting	b) Overhearing	c) Gossiping
11	a) butt in	b) grumble	c) gossip
12	a) chatting up	b) making eye contact	c) getting in touch

Past Simple and Present Perfect G1.1 G1.2

 2 Complete each pair of sentences with the same verb from the box. Use the Past Simple in one sentence and the Present Perfect Simple in the other.

be̶	make	hear	do	finish

1 a) I haven't seen her since we __were__ kids.
  b) I've hardly seen him since he __'s been__ unwell.

2 a) As soon as I .... any news from the hospital, I'll call you.
  b) As soon as I .... the noise, I knew it was an accident.

3 a) I .... my best to finish everything today, but by six o'clock I was shattered.
  b) I .... two exams today but there are still two more to do this afternoon.

4 a) We .... a lot of progress on the project this month, but the deadline isn't until the end of January.
  b) The company .... a little profit this month but it wasn't enough.

5 a) When she .... talking to Peter, we can have a quick meeting.
  b) When she .... talking to Peter, we had a quick meeting.

3 Read the interview. Choose the correct verb form.

Making a bad impression

Nancy Turnbull is the Director of Human Resources for a large multinational company. She ¹worked/has worked in human resources for large multinationals since 1990. She ²started/has started her first job when she left university and ³soon discovered/has soon discovered she had a talent for 'reading' people. During her time in the business, she estimates she ⁴saw/has seen over 3,000 potential candidates and probably 50 times as many CVs. So what makes a bad impression on her?

A lack of initiative
"As soon as the interview ⁵started/has started, I'll ask candidates the same question: 'What do you know about this company?' There's always a brochure about the company in reception. Last week a candidate ⁶waited/has waited for 20 minutes in reception before his interview. During that time, he ⁷did/has done nothing except stare out the window. Every company needs people who use 'dead' time as productively as possible."

A lack of clarity
"Sometimes a candidate ⁸talked/has been talking for quite some time and you realise you haven't really understood anything they've said since he or she ⁹was/has been in the room. Usually the problem is that they didn't understand the question when you ¹⁰asked/'ve asked it and they failed to ask you to explain further."

A lack of interest
"The most successful candidates that I ¹¹interviewed/'ve interviewed in my career have always made me feel like I was the one being interviewed! As soon as they've sat down, they ¹²asked/'ve asked me questions about the job and the company. They sound genuinely interested in the job – and not just the salary, of course!"

4 Read situations 1–5. Then use the prompts in brackets to write a sentence with the Past Simple or the Present Perfect Simple.

1 It's the afternoon. You started your homework this morning and by midday you were halfway through. Then you took a break for lunch.
   a) (I / finish / half of my homework so far.)

   ....

   b) (I / do / half of my homework this morning.) ....

   ....

2 Martin is company chairman. Sometimes he isn't popular, as he's trying to make the company profitable.
   a) (He's upset a lot of people since he / be / at the company.) ....

   ....

   b) (He's made a lot of changes since he / join / the company.) ....

   ....

3 Pablo and Maria started reading books in English in January. It's now November and they finished their fifth book today.
   a) (During the last year, they / read / five books in English.) ....

   ....

   b) (During the summer, they / read / two books in English.) ....

   ....

4 It's 1 p.m. Max went for three job interviews this morning, and he has another this afternoon. Amy went to one interview this morning.
   a) (Max / have / three interviews today.)

   ....

   b) (Amy / have / one interview this morning.) ....

   ....

5 Calvin passed his driving test last year. Since then, he's been saving for a car.
   a) (As soon as he / save up / enough money, he's going to buy a car.) ....

   ....

   b) (As soon as he / learn / to drive, he started saving.) ....

   ....

Prepositions and phrases V1.2

 1 a) Fill in gaps 1–3 with these prepositions.

~~in~~	out of	on

a) ....

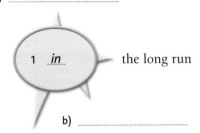

1 *in* — the long run

b) ....

c) ....

d) ....

2 .... — purpose

e) ....

f) ....

g) ....

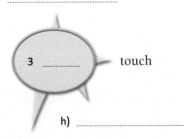

3 .... — touch

h) ....

i) ....

b) Fill in gaps a)–i) with these words/phrases.

a regular basis	your depth
the same wavelength	necessity
phases	average	touch
common	habit

 2 Replace the <u>underlined</u> words/phrases with prepositions and phrases from **1**.

in touch
My sister and I are good at staying [1]~~in communication with each other~~ and we speak on the phone reasonably [2]<u>regularly</u>. [3]<u>Typically</u>, one of us will phone perhaps once a fortnight. But I know that we usually do it [4]<u>without thinking about it</u> rather than because we really want to speak to each other. From time to time, I'll 'forget' to call her [5]<u>intentionally</u>, because I know we won't have much to say.

The problem is that we aren't [6]<u>similar in the way we think</u> at all and apart from our parents, we have little [7]<u>in the way of shared interests</u>. [8]<u>For short periods of time</u>, we sometimes might speak quite frequently. But that's usually [9]<u>because of a need</u>, for instance family things, rather than anything else. Occasionally, I'll call her for advice – for instance, when I feel [10]<u>I don't have the experience to deal</u> with something and I think she can help. I really hope we don't end up [11]<u>not speaking</u> with each other in the future.

Although I don't particularly worry about it now, I can imagine that [12]<u>after a long period of time</u>, we'll both probably regret it if we do.

Cleft sentences: *what* and *it* clauses G1.3

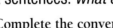 **3** Complete the conversations using the words in brackets.

1 A You're late. Did you run into bad traffic?
   B No, (I / home / left / what / my / happened / wallet / was / at)

   ....

   and had to go back.
2 A Aren't you hungry?
   B Not really, no. (What / late / lunch / a / I / had / was / happened)

   ....

   because I was in a meeting most of the day.
3 A Did you first meet your boyfriend at work?
   B No, (happened / was / he / chat up / tried / to / friend / my / what)

   ....

   in a bar but she was already seeing someone.
4 A Have you been in touch with Liz recently?
   B Not really. (of / periods / through / go / we / happens / is / What / daily / chatting) ....

   .... by email and then life gets busy again.
5 A Why are you and Tom always breaking up?
   B (happens / weeks / get on / a / for / few / well / What / is / we)

   ....

   and then we always fall out about something silly.

4 Complete b) so it has the same meaning as a).

1 a) I told him something. It was a secret.
   b) What I _____

2 a) I get on best with my aunt.
   b) The person _____

3 a) I'd like you to do something. Call me as soon as you get home.
   b) Something I'd _____

4 a) It annoyed me that she didn't call.
   b) The thing that _____

5 a) They're splitting up because of constant bickering.
   b) Their constant bickering _____

6 a) Those cars went out of fashion because they were environmentally unfriendly.
   b) The reason _____

7 a) This is what I did: I got in touch with all his friends.
   b) What I did _____

8 a) We grew up in this house.
   b) This house is _____

9 a) This is what happens: she witters on until I stop listening.
   b) What happens is _____

5 Rewrite sentence a) to emphasise the <u>underlined</u> information. Use *it + be + who/that*.

1 a) Liz hasn't been well for some time but <u>I only heard about it yesterday</u>.
   b) *Liz hasn't been well for some time but it was only yesterday that I heard about it.*

2 a) They say that women gossip a lot but the <u>men gossip more in our office</u>.
   b) They say that women gossip a lot but _____

3 a) I don't mind her rudeness but <u>her constant wittering gets on my nerves</u>.
   b) I don't mind her rudeness but _____

4 a) Nobody had told me anything so <u>I knew about the problem only by overhearing them</u>.
   b) Nobody had told me anything so _____

5 a) Everyone thinks Jane dumped her boyfriend but <u>he ended the relationship</u>.
   b) Everyone thinks Jane dumped her boyfriend but _____

6 a) I knew she wasn't happy but <u>I didn't realise how upset she was until you told me</u>.
   b) I knew she wasn't happy but _____

6 a) Correct the mistake in each sentence.

a) It are normally my sisters who I talk to about anything serious.
b) Then, what my brother does is to go upstairs and watch television.
c) What I really respect about they is that they are supportive in everything I do.
d) It's they that matter to me most.
e) What it happens is we get on well for about two days.
f) It's this year when is going to be the biggest challenge.

b) Fill in gaps 1–6 with the corrected sentences a)–f) from **6a**).

Friends or family?

" Without a doubt, my friends. I only see my family at Christmas – at my brother's house. ¹ _e)_ . On day three we start to bicker about little things. ² _____ . And we don't see him for the next six hours. ³ _____ . I've invited everyone to my house for a change! "

" I love my friends, of course. But I really love my family. ⁴ _____ . I'm really close to my parents and both of my sisters. ⁵ _____ . There are just some things you can't talk to your parents about. ⁶ _____ . "

Sayings V1.3

1 **a)** Make sayings with these words.

1 gained / Nothing / nothing / ventured .

....

2 twice / bitten / shy / Once .

....

3 man's / is / man's / One / meat / another / poison .

....

4 wasn't / Rome / day / a / in / built .

....

5 louder / Actions / than / speak / words .

....

6 out / mountain / a / make / Don't / molehill / a / of .

....

7 late / Better / never / than .

....

8 mouth / before / brain / Engage .

....

b) Complete these conversations with the most appropriate sayings from **1a)**.

1 A The next time he asks me to do 'a simple job', I'll know what to expect.
  B You will. _Once bitten, twice shy._

2 A I can't believe he didn't lock the door. We could have been burgled!
  B Well, we weren't. So ....

3 A I just butted in without thinking. And now she's really upset.
  B Well, ...

4 A I can't believe how long they've taken to redecorate. I just want to move in!
  B Be more patient. ....

5 A He's got all these ideas about building extensions and we end up doing nothing.
  B My husband's the same. I always tell him:

  ....

6 A I want to ask for a raise but what if he says "no"?
  B There's only one way you're going to find out. Remember: ....

7 A Personally, I couldn't stand working in an office.
  B Me neither. But she seems to like it. I guess

  ....

Explaining and paraphrasing RW1.1

2 Fill in the gaps with the phrases in the boxes.

> In other words   Which isn't to say that
> What I'm trying to say

JULIA It looks like our server's down. Did you know?

TOM Eh? You know I'm not technical, Julia.

JULIA Sorry. [1] .... is our website isn't working.

TOM Ah. OK. Call Softwire – they manage the website. The owner is Dan, but Phil's the brains behind the company. [2] .... Dan's unintelligent but …

JULIA [3] .... , I need to speak to Phil.

TOM Exactly.

> put it simply   what this means is   put it another

FIONA Economic conditions mean we need to make adjustments to the company. And [4] .... we need to cut costs.

MARK Or to [5] .... way, some of us are going to lose our jobs!

FIONA I'm afraid so. To [6] .... we need to make about eight people redundant.

> What I mean by that   Which is to
> Which basically means

MARIE I'm told you're a newspaper journalist. Who do you work for?

PAUL I'm freelance. [7] .... I work for everyone!

MARIE Everyone?

PAUL [8] .... is I write for lots of different newspapers and magazines.

MARIE Ah, is that like a temporary job?

PAUL Sort of. It's not unusual in my profession. [9] .... say lots of journalists are freelance.

● **Accurate Writing → 1 and 2 p84**

 Reading and Writing Portfolio 1 p54

2 Remarkable!

Language Summary 2, Student's Book p120

2A Exceptional people

Gradable and non-gradable adjectives; adverbs V2.1

1 Choose the correct words.

1 His achievement was *utterly/extremely* superb.
2 She's an *extremely/entirely* busy person.
3 The taste was *utterly/really* strong.
4 I felt *totally/slightly* tired.
5 Their story sounds *extremely/absolutely* awful.
6 Her knowledge of history is *fairly/utterly* huge.
7 I was *rather/fully* surprised by what he had done.
8 This exercise is *totally/very* impossible.

Intensifying adverbs V2.2

2 Read the article and choose the correct intensifying adverb.

	a)	b)	c)
1	deeply	thoroughly	strongly
2	completely	vividly	strongly
3	bitterly	highly	deeply
4	totally	extremely	bitterly
5	extremely	vividly	strongly
6	completely	deeply	firmly
7	thoroughly	quite	distinctly

3 Read sentence a). Then complete sentence b) with an intensifying adverb from box A and a verb from box B.

A really firmly distinctly completely deeply

B regrets believes enjoys agrees remembers

1 a) I love biographical films.
  b) He _____ _____ biographical films.
2 a) I think Martin's absolutely right.
  b) She _____ _____ with Martin.
3 a) I really wish I had listened to her advice.
  b) He _____ _____ not having listened to her advice.
4 a) I have a clear memory of meeting him.
  b) She _____ _____ meeting him.
5 a) In my opinion, creative talent in children must be encouraged.
  b) He _____ _____ in encouraging creative talent in children.

I may be exceptional but ...

Twice a year in the UK around 3,000 exceptional people are awarded a title, award or medal to reward aspects of charitable work, service to an industry or even a specific act of bravery.

Most people, of course, are delighted to receive recognition and [1] _____ enjoy seeing their names in the papers and meeting the Queen. However, every year, about 50 people refuse an award. Normally, these are kept secret but recently a list revealed over 300 famous people who have said "Thanks, but no thanks" to Her Majesty.

Some [2] _____ believe that the honours system is ridiculous. David Bowie, the musician, who turned down a knighthood in 2003, said "I seriously don't know what it's for." Having also refused a CBE (Commander of the British Empire) in 2000, it seems [3] _____ unlikely he will ever accept any honour.

Some people must have [4] _____ regretted refusing an award the first time because they later accepted one – examples include the author Graham Greene and the film director Alfred Hitchcock.

Others have been [5] _____ disappointed with their award and have refused it because they expected something better. Roald Dahl, the children's author, was offered an OBE (Officer of the Order of the British Empire) but wanted a knighthood so that his wife would get the title 'Lady Dahl'.

Many of the refusals, however, are at least in part a form of political protest. Stephen Hawking, the scientist, was [6] _____ frustrated with the government's attitude toward scientific funding over the years. Hence, he turned down his knighthood.

Clearly there are a variety of reasons why people might do this and not even good friends [7] _____ agree on the subject. Mick Jagger from the Rolling Stones is now 'Sir Mick' after accepting a knighthood in 2003. However, bandmate Keith Richards refused his CBE and said, "It's not what the [Rolling] Stones is about, is it?"

Relative clauses `G2.1`

4 Join these sentences, replacing each * with a relative clause. Make necessary changes.

1 An ex-soldier * has become the oldest person to be awarded a PhD by Cambridge University. He is 91 years old.

   An ex-soldier, who is 91 years old, has become the oldest

   person to be awarded a PhD by Cambridge University.

2 Colonel Michael Cobb's PhD * is called *The Railways of Great Britain: A Historical Atlas*. He began it in 1978.

3 The examiner * said, "It is a remarkable piece of scholarship." The examiner marked Michael's thesis.

4 The ceremony * will be attended by 40 members of Michael's family. It is being held in Cambridge.

5 Michael got his first degree at Cambridge at Magdalene College *. He studied mechanical sciences in the 1930s.

6 The Reverend Edgar Dowse * is the oldest person in the world to receive a PhD. He received his from Brunel University in 2004, aged 93.

Relative clauses with prepositions `G2.2`

5 a) Complete these sentences with *whom* or *which* and these phrases.

> ~~I applied required three years' experience~~
> I have great admiration   the Nobel Prize is named
> I complained was very tall   I invested went bust
> the film *Twenty-One* was based   he never came back

1 The job for ___which I applied required three years'___
   ___experience.___
2 My first teacher, Mr Turner, is someone for ___
3 The person to ___
4 He set off on a mission from ___
5 The business in ___
6 This is the book on ___
7 Dynamite was discovered by Alfred Nobel, after ___

b) Rewrite the sentences in **5a)** to be less formal.

1 *The job which I applied for required three years' experience.*
2 ___
3 ___
4 ___
5 ___
6 ___
7 ___

6 Make these sentences more formal by rewriting the phrases in **bold**, using relative clauses with prepositions.

   to which he confessed
1 The murder **which he confessed to** was merely one of his awful acts.
2 I would like to introduce someone **who I owe my life to**.
3 The person **who I was in correspondence with** seems to have left the company.
4 The day **that he died on** is now a national holiday.
5 His wife, **who he always collaborated with**, was at first given little credit for the discovery.
6 She loved charity work, **which her life was dedicated to**.
7 The room **which we are standing in** is where Anne wrote most of her diary.
8 The politician **who millions are protesting about** is a strong candidate for president.

7 Choose the correct words.

1 She's got three brothers, *one/all* of *which/whom* I went to school with. He was incredibly intelligent.
2 I'm a big fan of hers. She's released two albums as a solo artist, *both/most* of *which/whom* I've got on CD.
3 I can't stand where I work. My office is full of gossips, *neither/none* of *which/whom* I get on with.
4 He just isn't a very convincing actor. I've seen him in two films recently, *neither/both* of *which/whom* I've particularly enjoyed.
5 I'd read several of his books, *none/all* of *which/whom* I'd thoroughly enjoyed. So I was really looking forward to this one.
6 I was disappointed when I heard you weren't coming. However, Marta had invited over 50 people, *few/most* of *which/whom* I had met before.

2B Memorable places

Adjective word order

1 Complete the table with these adjectives.

| fur   middle-aged   turquoise   Northern European |
| ancient   phenomenal   frustrating   gigantic   West African |
| minuscule   beige   polyester   stainless steel   tiring |
| elderly   Mediterranean   pinkish   immense |

What do you think about it?	
How big is it?	
How old is it?	
What colour is it?	
Where is it from?	
What is it made of?	

2 Put these words in order and add *a/an*. Use the table in **1**.

1 clay / Moroccan / ancient / vase   *an ancient, Moroccan clay vase*
2 island / Atlantic / tiny / stunning ....
3 modern / inspiring / building / glass ....
4 peaceful / town / medieval / medium-sized ....
....
5 tropical / brownish / huge / fish ....
6 colour / beige / Victorian / inoffensive ....
7 material / greyish / stone / attractive ....

3 These phrases have too many adjectives. Rewrite them by putting the underlined in a separate clause using *with* or *in* or a relative pronoun.

1 a smart, young, <u>dark-haired and blue-eyed</u> man
   a smart young man with dark hair and blue eyes
2 a breathtaking, early, <u>signed and dated</u> painting by Picasso
....
3 a massive, old Italian <u>metal and wooden</u> sculpture
....
4 a miserable, tiny, one-bedroomed <u>70s-built</u> flat
....
5 a long, black, <u>white-buttoned</u> wool coat
....

Verb+*ing* and past participles

4 Correct the mistakes in these sentences.

1 I was a little worrying about calling her so late.
2 Can you listen for one minute without butt in?
3 I found the level of security on to enter the building quite worrying.
4 The prize, establish according to the wishes in Alfred Nobel's will, is awarded every year.
5 Passengers to leave on the 7.30 flight should be ready for embarkation at 7.00.
6 I can't help to gossip when I get bored at work.

Participle clauses   G2.4

5 These sentences are taken from a story you will read in **7**. Choose the correct connecting word.

1 *(As)/When* I waited for the kettle to boil in the kitchen at my office, I listened to everyone chatting over their coffee.
2 *Because/So* we were faced with a night sleeping in the car, we started the long journey home.
3 *While/After* we had rung numerous other places, and even a campsite, we were feeling more stressed than when we had left.
4 *When/After* we think about that weekend, even months later, we still fail to see the funny side.
5 We were bickering for over an hour, *when/so* we didn't notice how low we were on petrol.
6 We agreed a short break was a good idea, *so/because* we packed a small suitcase and set off on Saturday morning.
7 *So/If* you looked at it from the outside, the house looked fine.
8 *After/While* I overheard them swap plans, I couldn't help feeling a little envious.
9 The owner of the hotel was dressed entirely in black, *so/because* he didn't look the friendliest of hosts.
10 *Because/After* we hadn't thought that hotels would be full, we hadn't bothered to book anywhere.

6 Rewrite the sentences in **5** using a participle clause.

a) Waiting _for the kettle to boil in the kitchen at my office, I listened to everyone chatting over their coffee._

b) Faced ....

c) Having rung ....

d) ....

e) ....

f) ....

g) ....

h) ....

i) ....

j) ....

7 Read the story. Fill in gaps 1–10 with sentences a)–j) from **6**.

¹ _a)_ . The topic of conversation was holidays.
² .... My wife and I both had too much work to think about a long summer holiday. But what about a long weekend in the country? ³ .... By early afternoon, we were enjoying a picnic a few hours' drive from the busy city in which we live. Late in the afternoon, we started to think about somewhere to stay. ⁴ .... The nightmare began. We must have stopped at over ten hotels, none of which had any spare rooms. ⁵ .... Finally, we passed a small house with the sign 'Rooms Vacant' in the window. ⁶ .... However, once inside, we started to feel distinctly nervous. ⁷ .... Our room, which clearly hadn't been occupied for some time, was filthy. Within a quarter of an hour we were back in the car again. ⁸ .... But the nightmare wasn't over. ⁹ .... Eventually the car stopped and we realised what was wrong. To cut a long story short, we got home at around 6 a.m. on Sunday morning and slept the entire day. ¹⁰ ....

8 Complete these sentences with a present participle, a past participle or a perfect participle (*Having* + past participle). Use the verbs in the box.

play	lose	wake up	flick
serve	look after	spend	need

1 .... three months in Poland as a child, I knew how hot it could get in the summer.

2 Even .... on an old record player, records can sound richer than CDs.

3 .... through a glossy magazine, I came across an article on responsible tourism.

4 .... some time alone, he headed off to the country.

5 .... with ice, crushed limes and sugar, it's a refreshing drink.

6 .... at dawn and been unable to get back to sleep, I decided to go exploring.

7 .... my passport before, I knew how terrible she felt.

8 .... carefully, furniture of this quality should last you a lifetime.

9 These sentences have a different subject in each clause. Rewrite the underlined clauses so that the meaning is clear.

1 The Argentinian hotel owner and I were able to communicate, having studied Spanish at school.
I was able to communicate with the Argentinian hotel owner, having studied Spanish at school.

2 Not looking where he was going, the car knocked him down.

....

....

3 Watching the rain from the safety of our hotel room, the street soon became flooded.

....

....

4 Butting in every five minutes, I became deeply frustrated with Jenny's arrogance.

....

....

5 Michael made me feel unappreciated, having worked day and night on the report.

....

....

Adjectives: describing places V2.4

1 Replace the underlined with these words.

> ~~meandering~~   golden   unspoilt   medieval
> unique   cosmopolitan   diverse

a) Whether you are seeking historical adventure, cultural entertainment or simply solitude and peace in a <u>directionless and purposeless</u> tour through the highlands, the country offers a wealth of attractions. _meandering_

b) In the latter, the <u>dating from 600AD to 1500AD</u> Edinburgh Castle dominates the skyline perched on top of an extinct volcano. _____

c) One of their main attractions are the <u>unusual and special</u> prehistoric standing stones. _____

d) Northern Scotland is one of the most <u>unchanged and undamaged</u> parts of Britain. _____

e) In fact, it has some of the most stunning <u>yellow in colour</u> stretches of sand in the world. _____

f) Its <u>varied and different</u> and spectacular scenery ranges from the Highlands to the moors and lochs _____

g) Glasgow and Edinburgh, Scotland's capital, are the two largest and most <u>international</u> cities. _____

Reading

2 Read the website and fill in gaps 1–7 with a)–g) from **1**.

3 Read again. Are these sentences true (T), false (F) or the website doesn't say (DS)?

1 ☐ Edinburgh Castle is Scotland's most popular tourist attraction.

2 ☐ The Orkneys have only been inhabited in recent times.

3 ☐ St Andrews has a long tradition of golf.

4 ☐ Loch Ness is the largest Scottish lake.

5 ☐ Scotland has surprisingly good weather.

6 ☐ Scotland's best art gallery is in Glasgow.

• **Accurate Writing** → 3 and 4 p84

 Reading and Writing Portfolio 2 p57

---

http://www.enjoyscotland.net/home

There are few places with the combination of breathtaking natural scenery and numerous historical sites that Scotland offers. ¹ _____ .

Feeling the need to get away from it all? The Orkneys are a group of islands just off the northeast coast of mainland Scotland. ² _____ that reflect the long history of these isolated and serene locations.

The Orkney Islands

to the Shetland Islands

NORTHERN SCOTLAND

☐ ● Inverness
Loch Ness

CENTRAL SCOTLAND

☐
Ben Nevis

☐ St Andrew's

Edinburgh

● Glasgow

SOUTHERN SCOTLAND

³ _____ . It stretches from Ben Nevis, the highest mountain in Great Britain, to the windswept Shetland islands, some 150 kilometres from the most northern tip of Scotland. ⁴ _____ including, of course, Loch Ness.

With its reputation for temperamental and unforgiving weather, you may have assumed Scotland is devoid of beaches. ⁵ _____ . St Andrews, on the east coast in Central Scotland, and the home of golf, boasts broad beaches which famously featured in the opening sequence of the Oscar-winning film *Chariots of Fire*.

Known as the lowlands, Southern Scotland is the most populated area of the country. ⁶ _____ . In the former, the Kelvingrove Art Gallery is the country's premier museum and art gallery, housing works by, among others, Dalí, Rembrandt and Botticelli. ⁷ _____ .

3 Well-being

Language Summary 3, Student's Book p124

3A Being confident

Positive character adjectives V3.1

1 What character adjective is each question asking about? Complete the crossword.

Across (→)

1 It's late and you're in bed and you hear a noise downstairs. Would you go down and investigate?
4 You've failed your driving test three times and the lessons are costing you a fortune. Would you try a fourth time?
5 Your decorators can only come when you are at work. Would you give them a key?
7 It's very late and you have just finished a report at work which you need to give to your boss tomorrow morning. You know you need to read it through one last time. Would you do it?
8 You arrive at a restaurant and everyone is dressed more smartly than you. Would you stay or go home and change?

Down (↓)

1 You've been searching unsuccessfully for your wallet for a few hours but you're sure it's in the house. Would you cancel your credit cards?
2 You suddenly receive a large bonus at work and you know your best friend needs some money. Would you give him/her anything?
3 It's Friday. Your best friend has just won two tickets abroad for the weekend and wants you to go. Would you go?
6 You're having a good time at a party and the last bus home leaves soon. After that, you would have to get a taxi. Would you leave now?

Connotation: positive and negative character adjectives V3.2

2 Complete 1–9 with these character adjectives.

~~reckless~~	extravagant	tight-fisted	gullible
arrogant	finicky	obstinate	timid	impetuous

1 You might think what you did was brave but I see it as _reckless_ . You could have been seriously injured.
2 I've never seen Jim compromise about anything. He's the most _____ person I've ever worked with.
3 I don't understand how some people believe a random email telling them they've won a lottery they never even bought a ticket for! How _____ is that?
4 I wish you wouldn't be so _____ with presents. I can't afford to give you expensive things and I feel so embarrassed.
5 Our cat's so _____ she rarely goes outdoors!
6 We made too much fuss over our kids and food. Now they're teenagers they're terribly _____ about what they eat.
7 I used to be _____ but I've learned to think carefully about decisions and their consequences.
8 Isabel failed the exam but I find it hard to feel sorry for her. She's so _____ , she hardly did any revision.
9 I'd like to say my father is careful with his money but in fact, he's just _____ .

3 Match each negative adjective in **2** with the more positive adjectives from **1**.

1 _____ _reckless_ — _courageous_
2 _____ — _____
3 _____ — _____
4 _____ — _____
5 _____ — _____
6 _____ — _____
7 _____ — _____
8 _____ — _____
9 _____ — _____

Introductory *it* G3.1

4 Rewrite these sentences using introductory *it* + verb + adjective.

1 That they weren't fired was very fortunate.

....

2 Grumbling to your boss is pointless.

....

3 That the meetings are arranged this week is imperative.

....

4 Working with someone so demanding can be difficult.

....

5 To assume he would be safe alone in the house was wholly arrogant.

....

6 That only a few weeks ago she had no experience is astounding.

....

5 **a)** Read the first part of the article. Fill in gaps 1–6 with introductory *it* and the correct form of the verbs from A and phrases from B.

┌─────────────────────────────────────┐
│ **A** ~~turn out~~   not be   emerge │
│   frighten   be   surprise   │
└─────────────────────────────────────┘

┌─────────────────────────────────────┐
│ **B** ~~that she was just tight-fisted~~ │
│   not a situation that continued for long │
│   everyone to see him lose his temper │
│   that he was going through a messy divorce │
│   me to see her get out   │
│   something I'd ever want to experience │
└─────────────────────────────────────┘

b) Read the second part of the article. Fill in gaps 7–12 with the correct form of the verbs in A + introductory *it* and phrases from B.

┌─────────────────────────────────────┐
│ **A** ~~not mind~~   can't bear   resent   prefer │
│   not find   find   │
└─────────────────────────────────────┘

┌─────────────────────────────────────┐
│ **B** when I came into the office after the weekend │
│   difficult to understand at all   │
│   when she was offered the job   │
│   ~~when people make a mistake and admit it~~ │
│   funny to ask people the time   │
│   when the office was more boring   │
└─────────────────────────────────────┘

Colleagues from hell!

We asked people to tell us about the worst people they've worked with …

I once offered my neighbour lifts to work because we work in the same office. I knew she had a reputation for being thrifty, but ¹ *it turned out that she was just tight-fisted* ! After the first week, I expected her to offer something towards my petrol costs. However, on Friday night, as I dropped her off in front of her house, ² .... and wave goodbye without a word – not even a 'thank you'. Fortunately, ³ .... I got a new job about a month later – nowhere near my old office.

I used to have a nightmare boss – he was terribly obstinate at times. And when he didn't get his own way, you knew it was going to be a bad day. ⁴ ....

He would shout at people and storm out of meetings, slamming the door behind him. He eventually got fired for his behaviour and later ⁵ .... Looking back on the situation, I feel sorry for him. ⁶ ....

⁷I *don't mind it when people make a mistake and admit it* . However, I once had a colleague who was totally incompetent and nothing was ever her fault. Then one day she applied for a managerial position in another department. A lot of people ⁸ .... Someone even made a complaint but it didn't make any difference. Personally, I ⁹ .... There are plenty of fools in management already!

I had a colleague once who was a real 'joker'. She ⁶ .... when they were carrying cups of coffee. I lost count of the number of times I saw people pour drinks on their shoes. I ¹¹ .... She'd always arrived early and would have done something 'amusing'. Once she plugged the keyboards on our computers into different machines. Hilarious. Some people thought she had really livened up our department. I ¹² .... She was such an idiot!

3B   A happy, healthy life

Phrasal verbs: health V3.3

 1 Tick (✓) the correct sentences. Then correct the mistakes.

1 I got stung by a wasp on my arm and it started to swell it up.
2 There's some kind of flu going around that everyone's going down with.
3 He's got some kind of food poisoning – he must have picked up it on holiday.
4 Helen picked up a cold a few weeks ago and she still hasn't got it over yet.
5 I'm taking some drugs which the doctor put me on.
6 My nose has been blocked up for over a month!
7 She came out on a rash after eating some shellfish.

2 Read the email and rewrite the underlined phrases using the correct form of these phrasal verbs.

put on	go down with	swell up	get over
come out in	go around	pick up	not be blocked up

☒

Hi Sue,

Sorry I haven't emailed in a while. I've been ¹recovering from flu – again! You warned me that having a young baby would be like this and you were right. There always seems to be some kind of illness ²being passed around Eveline's nursery and within a few days she ³catches it. And then all of us ⁴become ill with the same thing. I can't remember the last time my nose ⁵was clear!

To top it all, in the showers at swimming on Saturday, I noticed that ⁶spots had appeared on Eveline. Chicken pox! Fortunately, I had it long ago but Clare, poor thing, hadn't and by Sunday it was clear she'd got it too. We read on the Internet that it is quite dangerous for adults and terrifyingly, it can cause the brain to ⁷get larger! Anyway, she saw the doctor yesterday and he didn't seem concerned – though he ⁸has given her some kind of anti-viral drugs.

Anyway, how are you? I'm in your area in a few weeks so maybe we could meet up for lunch? Assuming Clare and Eveline are better, of course.

Dino x

Subject and verb inversion G3.2

 3 Complete the sentences with the correct phrase from these pairs.

> ~~she might have~~/might she have   I've met/have I met
> So do I/It does me, too   So I am/So am I
> has she gone down/she's gone down
> Here she comes/Here comes she
> There goes the man/There the man goes
> Neither am I/Neither I am

1 Have you any idea where __she might have__ picked it up?
2 A I'm not feeling too good.
   B ....
3 A I don't know where the assistant has gone.
   B .... We can ask her now.
4 Never .... someone who wittered on so much.
5 A I'm coming down with something, I think.
   B .... I've been feeling awful all day.
6 I wonder if .... with the same thing I had.
7 .... I told you about. He was really rude to me.
8 A It annoys me when people take the week off just because of a cold.
   B ....

 4 Fill in the gaps with one or two words.

1 I can't stand going on diets and .... my husband. However, we both enjoy running.
2 She asked me if .... the time. I told her it was around half past two.
3 A Look! .... the bus. Have you got your ticket ready?
   B Yes, but I don't think that's our bus.
4 A I'm getting a bit overweight, ... ?
   B A little, perhaps.
5 I love green vegetables and fortunately, ... both of my children.
6 A Have you any idea what .... arriving?
   B He should be here around six.

Inversion G3.3

 a) Rewrite these sentences.

a) I only give in and have one when it's a special occasion.

Only when ....

b) Restaurants have only recently started to print nutritional information on their menus.

Only recently ....

c) I don't decide which restaurant to go to till I've satisfied myself there are some healthy options.

Not until ....

d) You should never feel forced to have a starter and a main course.

On no account ....

e) I almost never order something without asking for it to be changed in some way.

Seldom ....

f) People almost never eat out as healthily as they should.

Rarely ....

g) I didn't really realise how much sugar is added to these drinks.

Little ....

h) It will slow you down and also help you enjoy your food more.

Not only ....

b) Read the article. Fill in gaps 1–8 with the rewritten sentences from 5a).

 Rewrite these sentences using the phrases in the box.

| Not only   Seldom   In no way   Not until   Nowhere   Only on |

1 You won't find better food anywhere.

....

2 It's greasy *and* tastes of nothing.

....

3 We only eat out on special occasions.

....

4 People don't often eat as many vegetables as they should.

....

5 We didn't know how expensive it was going to be till we got the bill.

....

6 Burgers could never be described as healthy.

....

Staying healthy while eating out

[1] .... **. There are just too many tempting things on the menu. But it is possible. And here are some simple tips that might help.**

- Eating out is not the time for being a timid consumer. [2] .... For example, instead of chips, I might request a baked potato or if something is fried, I'll ask for it to be grilled. Be assertive!

- [3] .... However, this can be misleading. If something is low in carbohydrates, it isn't necessarily low in fat.

- Many restaurants with a website include a menu with information about ingredients. [4] ....

- I used to love a cocktail before my meal. Then someone told me how unhealthy they were. [5] .... Now I have a small glass of wine or a light beer.

- Give your brain time to realise your stomach is full and drink plenty of water during your meal. [6] ....

- [7] .... If the starters have a bigger range of healthy dishes, order two of these instead.

- Skip desserts. [8] .... 'Triple Chocolate Mountain Meltdown' may sound delicious but it will probably treble the calories in your entire meal.

3C It's the way you say it

Euphemisms V3.4

1 Correct the underlined idioms.

getting on a bit

Now I'm ¹~~going up a bit~~ I often feel ²<u>below the time</u> when I listen to my grandchildren talking to each other – especially the teenagers. They seem to talk in a different language! It doesn't

help that I'm a little ³<u>hard to hear</u> too. When I ask them to explain what they're talking about, I always get the funny feeling that they're being a little ⁴<u>efficient on the truth</u>. Anyway, I expect I was the same at their age!

The youngest ones are simpler. I've got two three-year-old grandsons – twins – and although they can be ⁵<u>a bit of an armful</u>, I love spending time with them. At 75, I'm officially a ⁶<u>superior citizen</u> which means I can travel on public transport in Britain for free. This is really useful as our car has ⁷<u>seen healthier times</u> and I was finding driving and parking quite ⁸<u>determining</u>. Apart from my hearing, my health is reasonably good. From time to time, I feel ⁹<u>below the climate</u> but it usually passes within a day or two. I do feel the cold more than I used to. I have the heating on quite a lot as otherwise, the house gets ¹⁰<u>a bit at the chilling side</u>. My teenage grandchildren always say my house is like a sauna!

Being tactful RW3.1

2 **a)** Make sentences with these words.

a) you / looser / better / pair / I / would / think / suit / a .

....

b) could / a / detailed / it / Frankly, / been / more / have / bit .

....

c) night / early / an / get / to / planning / was / I .

....

d) was / It / side / short / the / on / bit / a .

....

e) better / seen / I've / designs .

....

f) you / were / I / if / down / it / turn / I'd .

....

g) interesting / times / was / of / at / It / sort .

....

h) It / louder / bit / a / being / with / do / could .

....

b) Fill in the gaps with sentences a)–h) from 2a).

1 A Do my legs look fat in these?
  B ....

2 A Honestly, what did you think of my speech?
  B Very funny! .... But then again, people do get bored when they go on.

3 A What did you think of that article I sent you?
  B .... But it went on too long.

4 A What do you think of my new mobile?
  B .... Or perhaps I'm getting a bit hard of hearing!

5 A Do you think the music is too loud?
  B .... It's quite late.

6 A Do you fancy going out for a drink later?
  B Sorry. .... It's been a challenging week, to say the least.

7 A What did you think of their new kitchen?
  B .... I mean the cupboards didn't look particularly strong, did they?

8 A Did you manage to read my report? Sorry it was quite short.
  B Yes. .... You had a month to prepare.

● **Accurate Writing →** 5 and 6 p85

Reading and Writing Portfolio 3 p60

4 Civilised

4A Society and the media

News collocations V4.1

 1 Read the guide to handling publicity and choose the best word to fill in the gaps.

How to stay famous by using the press

- Read all the tabloids and the ¹_____ magazines every day? Can you find something about you that isn't quite true? If you can, ²_____ a press ³_____ and tell people how hurt you are by what has been written about you. And then announce your intention to ⁴_____ for libel.

- It's almost always good to ⁵_____ the headlines, but you don't want to ⁶_____ the ⁷_____ page too often. The public will become bored if you ⁸_____ too much ⁹_____ .

- Make a large and 'anonymous' charitable donation. And then make sure the tabloids ¹⁰_____ a ¹¹_____ about you being the 'anonymous' donor. ¹²_____ a press ¹³_____ immediately, saying that you wish no one knew about it. After all, you say, never ¹⁴_____ publicity.

1	a) sparkly	b) shiny	c) glossy
2	a) grab	b) hold	c) take
3	a) reunion	b) meeting	c) conference
4	a) charge	b) arrest	c) sue
5	a) hit	b) strike	c) punch
6	a) create	b) do	c) make
7	a) face	b) front	c) first
8	a) deliver	b) collect	c) receive
9	a) treatment	b) coverage	c) reporting
10	a) run	b) produce	c) make
11	a) tale	b) story	c) chronicle
12	a) Issue	b) Provide	c) Give out
13	a) release	b) statement	c) comment
14	a) hunt	b) take	c) seek

Future verb forms G4.1

2 Choose the correct answers. If there is more than one correct answer, what is the difference in meaning?

1 Did you know _____ a press conference today?
   a) he's holding   b) he's going to hold   c) he'll hold
   Difference: _____

2 We _____ a press release as soon as reporters from the tabloids are here.
   a) 'll be issuing   b) 'll have issued   c) issue
   Difference: _____

3 Those glossy magazines are just full of celebrity trivia. I know. I _____ buying them.
   a) 'm going to stop   b) am stopping   c) 'll stop
   Difference: _____

4 Do you think it _____ the front page?
   a) will make   b) will be making   c) makes
   Difference: _____

5 We can't run this story. I _____ time to check the facts.
   a) won't have   b) 'm not having   c) won't have had
   Difference: _____

6 The story is completely untrue and _____ them for libel.
   a) he'll have sued   b) he'll sue   c) he's going to sue
   Difference: _____

7 They _____ happy seeing their names all over the papers.
   a) won't be   b) aren't being   c) won't be being
   Difference: _____

Phrases referring to the future G4.2

3 Tick (✓) the headlines that talk about a future event.

1 **PRINCE ABOUT TO MARRY AGAIN?** ✓ _____

2 INFLATION TO GO BEYOND 4% SOON _____

3 ENERGY PRICE RISE DUE TO 'ARROGANCE OF MINISTERS' _____

4 **LIBEL ACTION SUCCESSFUL – THOUSANDS SET TO BENEFIT £500+** _____

5 **MINISTER ACCEPTS APOLOGY FROM NEWSPAPER** _____

6 **ENGLAND MANAGER DUE TO ISSUE PRESS RELEASE** _____

7 GOVERNMENT ON VERGE OF CRISIS TALKS _____

4 Rewrite headlines 1–7 in **3** as full sentences. There is sometimes more than one possible answer.

1   *Is the prince about to get married again?*

2   ....

3   ....

4   ....

5   ....

6   ....

7   ....

5 Read the stories and choose the correct future phrases.

Some people feel that the newspaper industry is on the
¹*point/brink of/verge* complete collapse and that within ten
years, we are ²*sure/about/due* to get our entire news diet from
the Internet and television. While the popularity of online news
³*is bound to/is likely/certain* rise, it does not necessarily follow
that readers are ⁴*due/likely to/on the point of* abandon
newspapers altogether.

Since interest rates ⁵*be certain/certain/are certain* to rise again
next month, politicians ⁶*are hold/to hold/are to hold* an
emergency summit on the economic problems. The topic
⁷*is set/is unlikely/due* to get so much coverage that newspaper
editors must be on the verge of ⁸*order/to order/ordering* extra
paper for their morning print runs.

6 Rewrite these sentences using one of the phrases in brackets.

1 We launch our new website next month. (*set to/~~sure to~~*)

   We're set to launch our new website next month.

2 We probably won't finish before July. (*unlikely to/not due to*)

   ....

3 They're publishing a new edition very soon.
   (*bound to/about to*)

   ....

4 He will almost certainly be late. (*bound to/set to*)

   ....

5 Their new album will definitely be a success.
   (*on the verge of/certain to*)

   ....

6 We're landing at 5.30. (*bound to/due to*)

   ....

7 Her business is going bust in the near future.
   (*verge of/likely to*)

   ....

7 Fill in the gaps with the correct form of these phrases.

~~about to / hold~~	~~be / answer~~
sure / include	unlikely / be
set / grow	due / take place
likely / face	verge / complete
sure / take	verge / quit

1 The actor is *about to hold* a press
   conference about his court appearance
   where he *is to answer* a charge of
   dangerous driving.

2 Space tourism .... at a
   significant rate over the new few decades
   and all the major airlines ....
   .... an interest.

3 The Prime Minister ....
   say several insiders. However, whatever
   happens over the next few weeks, the
   government .... a
   difficult election in May.

4 The Brazilian player ....
   his transfer to the Premiership club. The
   list of his demands ....
   a weekly salary of nearly £200,000.

5 A vote on the new law ....
   .... at the House of
   Lords this evening. However, as
   opposition is growing daily, it
   .... successful.

8 Tick (✓) the correct sentences. Then correct the mistakes.

1 The actor set to be the star and director
   of the third part in the series.

2 Crying quietly, she was on the verge of
   tearing up her application.

3 The newspaper, about to celebrate its
   100th birthday, is due to close.

4 The stories likely to receive more
   publicity over the coming months.

5 The amount, is due to be announced this
   week, is believed to be triple the estimate.

6 Markets are on the verge of collapse.

7 I definitely won't have finished it by the
   time he's arriving.

8 The new stadium will have been build
   by 2011.

4B Cities and technology

Near synonyms V4.2

 a) Read the first part of this article about mobile phones. Fill in gaps 1–6 with these words/phrases.

> ~~most recent~~   rising   people   former
> focused   concept

According to the [1] _most recent_ figures, the 'adoption rate' of mobile phones in the USA is 85%. That's higher than both the percentage of [2] _____ who have DVD players (84%) or computers (80%).

"The [3] _____ that within my lifetime we'd have the kind of penetration we have today is unimaginable," says Martin Cooper, 79, the [4] _____ Motorola researcher who invented the portable cell phone in 1973.

But it's not all good news for mobile phone companies. To keep revenues [5] _____, the big carriers are [6] _____ mostly on stealing each other's existing customers and getting mobile users to spend more on ringtones, streaming music and other add-ons.

b) Replace words/phrases 1–6 in **1a)** with these words/phrases.

> ~~latest~~   idea   on the increase
> ex-   concentrating   consumers

1 _latest_   4 _____
2 _____   5 _____
3 _____   6 _____

2 Read the second part of the article. Match eight pairs of near synonyms from the <u>underlined</u> words/phrases.

The bulk of the 'un-mobile' – that is, people without mobile phones – fall into three groups, namely: <u>children</u>, the elderly and the credit-challenged. (There's actually a fourth crowd – prison inmates – but companies haven't <u>yet</u> found <u>ways</u> to target them!)

Parents aren't <u>sure</u> about their <u>kids</u> having mobile phones – <u>especially</u> because they pay the <u>bill</u>. Nevertheless, <u>figures</u> suggest that <u>so far</u> half of the USA's 28 million 8- to 14-year-olds have their own <u>handsets</u>.

Fear of an enormous <u>demand for payment</u> also concerns the elderly. But increasingly, they are <u>convinced</u> it's good to have a phone for emergencies.

For consumers without bank accounts, prepaid <u>phones</u> have been a <u>particularly</u> popular alternative to having a contract. Lately, charges have come down significantly and companies now offer a better variety of phones and numerous <u>methods</u> of putting credit on the phone. As a result, <u>numbers</u> indicate that prepaid phones are the fastest-growing segment of the market.

a) _children; kids_   e) _____
b) _____   f) _____
c) _____   g) _____
d) _____   h) _____

Future in the past G4.3

3 Choose the most appropriate ending for each sentence.

1 I was about to go home …
   a) and arrived just in time.
   b) when I realised I didn't have any keys.

2 We were going to move out of London …
   a) but then Ruth was offered a great job in the City.
   b) and we are looking for somewhere near the coast.

3 Rick and I were supposed to be going out that night …
   a) and I was really looking forward to it.
   b) so I had a really good time.

4 It was to take five years to complete the building …
   a) and it was never completed.
   b) and it would be opened by the Prime Minister himself.

5 I thought it would be impossible to buy a house …
   a) so I expect I'll always be renting.
   b) but somehow I did.

6 I wasn't going to tell you yet …
   a) so don't ask me again.
   b) but I can't keep the news secret any longer.

4 Read the article about predictions. Then fill in the gaps with these phrases.

| would be needed   wouldn't have   was to see |
| were supposed to be   weren't we going to be |
| would pass   were about to have |

Hasn't the future been disappointing? We're already well into the 21st century but it doesn't feel like it.

According to Henry Ford's prediction made in 1940, we ¹ _____ whizzing around in flying cars by the 1950s. My vehicle is still firmly stuck to the road. About 15 years ago we ² _____ our lives revolutionised by 'virtual reality'. There's nothing 'virtual' about my reality, I'm afraid. And it's not very revolutionary. And finally, by the turn of the century, ³ _____ living on the moon? I'm happy here on Earth but it would be comforting to know there is an alternative.

However, there's a fortunate side to the unreliability of predictions, too. In the 1970s it was predicted that just five computers ⁴ _____ worldwide. Now, in the USA for example, 80% of households own one. For many of my generation, life without the Internet is unthinkable.

Even Alexander Bell somewhat underestimated the success of his 'telephone'. His dream was that "One day, there will be a telephone in every American city." Before he died in 1922, he ⁵ _____ over a million of his most famous invention in use all over the world.

Worst of all, according to the *New York Times* in 1939, the average US family ⁶ _____ time for this new thing called 'television' and that soon this craze ⁷ _____ . Imagine: instead of slumping in front of the box every evening, I would have had to read a book – or even talk to my parents!

As a wise man once said, "Prediction is very difficult, especially if it's about the future."

5 Fill in the gaps with the correct form of the words/phrases in brackets and a verb from the box. You do not need to change the form of the verbs in the box.

| run   say   speak   get   discover   tell |
| be delivered   finish   drive   turn |

1 Nobody imagined that one day he _would run_ the whole company. (would)
2 I'm sorry I butted in. _____ you _____ something? (be about to)
3 They _____ all the building work by Monday as that's when the painters were coming. (be supposed to)
4 We _____ years later that we'd been living next door to a criminal. (be to)
5 Your present _____ last week but I think it's got lost. (be supposed to)
6 I _____ to Mark's house but it looks like Clare's taken my keys. (be going to)
7 It's lucky you warned me as I _____ him everything. (be about to)
8 I thought I _____ here on time but I found a shortcut to avoid the traffic. (wouldn't)
9 I _____ to him many more times before his death in 2006. (be to)
10 Computers _____ offices into paperless environments but it hasn't happened here! (be going to)

6 Rewrite the phrases in **bold** using the words in brackets.

1 **I had planned to call him very soon** but then you rang. (about to)

   I was about to call him but then you rang.

2 We **had arranged a meeting** at one o'clock but she didn't turn up. (supposed)

   _____

3 **It was my intention** to leave early and get the four o'clock train. (going)

   _____

4 **Hadn't you intended** to be working at home today? (supposed)

   _____

5 The train was **on the verge of leaving** when we arrived. (about to)

   _____

6 We **intended making** our final decision that evening. (going)

   _____

Making a splash

Reading

 Read articles A and B quickly. Then answer the questions.

Which article ...

1 uses slang? __B__
2 has longer sentences? _____
3 uses more emotive language? _____
4 has a more dramatic headline? _____
5 uses more phrasal verbs? _____
6 has the most information about the incident? _____
7 uses more complex language? _____
8 has asked a wider range of people to comment? _____
9 is from a tabloid newspaper? _____
10 is from a broadsheet newspaper? _____

'Mindless' biker puts 189mph ride on Internet

A motorcyclist who filmed himself ¹reaching 189mph on a Cotswolds road and then ²posted the ³footage on a website was ⁴condemned as ⁵"mindless and arrogant" by road safety campaigners.

The ⁶unidentified biker made the video of himself ⁷riding down the A417 near Cirencester. He had mounted a camera on the front of his motorbike so it could record the speedometer.

It is believed that 189mph is the highest speed recorded on a British road and is the maximum of the Kawasaki ZX-10R being used.

The three-minute video clip then appeared on YouTube but has since been ⁸removed from the site.

Gary Handley, the Gloucestershire Road Safety Group team leader, said: "If anything had gone wrong, the outcome would have been catastrophic for [the biker] and quite possibly other drivers. The driver was sharing the road with other vehicles and negotiating roundabouts."

Inspector David Collicott, of Gloucester police, said: "The public roads are not the place to practice or display this type of driving and the YouTube clip does nothing to help prevent this type of recklessness being perpetuated."

Investigations to identify the driver are continuing.

Reckless rider reaches 189mph and puts vid on YouTube!

A ROAD SAFETY charity has slammed a reckless biker who filmed himself roaring down a dual carriageway at 189mph – and then put the clip on YouTube.

The video – by user Adrenalinetwist – shows a clip of the speed dial on a Kawasaki ZX-10R as it clocks up a mind-blowing 189mph.

The speed freak forces other drivers to change lanes as he powers in the direction of the A417 Swindon to Gloucester road.

The bike is also seen weaving dangerously in and out of traffic on a single carriageway in an urban area.

And at one point, the video cuts to a shot taken from the side of the road as the motorbike screams past.

Road safety charity Brake slammed the mysterious driver's recklessness.

A spokesperson said, "This guy is putting other road users in danger, going way in excess of the speed limit on that road.

"It's putting the message out that this is a fun thing to do, which is not the case. YouTube needs to get this clip off its site."

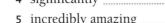 Look at <u>underlined</u> words/phrases 1–8 in article A. Find a word/phrase in article B which has a similar meaning. Sometimes there is more than one possible answer.

1 _as it clocks up_   5 _____
2 _____   6 _____
3 _____   7 _____
4 _____   8 _____

 Find words/phrases in article B which match these definitions.

1 travelling quickly and changing direction to avoid hitting things _____
2 someone who likes driving or travelling fast _____
3 moves very quickly making a loud high noise _____
4 significantly _____
5 incredibly amazing _____

4 Underline the following information in the articles. Does it come from article A, article B or both?

1 how the biker made his film
2 where the biker was travelling
3 who commented on the video
4 how long the video clip was
5 what the bike's top speed was

 ● **Accurate Writing** → 7 and 8 p85

Reading and Writing Portfolio 4 p63

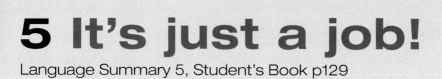

5 It's just a job!
Language Summary 5, Student's Book p129

5A Behind the glamour

Word building (1): prefixes with multiple meanings V5.1

1 Complete each pair of sentences with the same prefix from box A and a different word from box B.

A	counter	super	inter	over	under	semi

B	~~clockwise~~	head	staffed	rated	-detached
	-attack	sweet	locking	ground	computers
	-darkness	action			

1 a) You always rotate screws __counterclockwise__ to undo them.
  b) With only ten men, and trying desperately for an equaliser, Manchester United were always in danger of _____ .

2 a) Our house is _____ , which means it is easy for burglars to get into the back garden.
  b) In the _____ of the evening, I couldn't quite make out who it was.

3 a) Please put your hand luggage either in the _____ lockers or beneath your seats.
  b) I've never seen such an _____ film – I can't understand how it got such rave reviews.

4 a) Modern games consoles such as the Playstation 3, are over 100 times more powerful than the so-called '_____' devised less than 20 years ago.
  b) I love those oranges – I think they call them '_____' or something like that.

5 a) The property includes use of a secure _____ car park which is monitored by 24-hour CCTV.
  b) We are terribly _____ at the moment, which is the reason for our delay in replying.

6 a) He used a type of _____ flooring where the pieces of wood fit into each other to prevent movement.
  b) My last job involved a lot of _____ with the public, so I'm used to meeting all kinds of people.

2 Match the use of the prefixes in each sentence in **1** to meanings a)–l).

a) in opposition to __counterclockwise__
b) not enough _____
c) half _____
d) too much _____
e) as a reaction to _____
f) better than usual _____
g) joined together _____
h) extremely _____
i) from above/on top/across _____
j) partly _____
k) between (people, etc.) _____
l) below _____

Reflexive pronouns (1) G5.1

3 Choose the correct word/phrase. Sometimes both answers are correct.

1 No one wanted to help me so I did it *myself/by myself*.
2 The two chemicals react with *each other/themselves* to produce a dangerous and highly volatile compound.
3 The company largely takes care of *it/itself* and there isn't much for me to do any more.
4 She was so pleased with *her/herself* that she gave *her/herself* the afternoon off.
5 You can't blame *you/yourselves* for what happened.
6 I watched them walk past *each other/themselves* without saying a word.
7 He took time out of filming to say hello to John and *me/myself*.
8 We seem to have no time to *us/ourselves* these days.
9 The manager of the company phoned *me/myself*.
10 I should have known – if you want something done properly, you have to do it *by yourself/yourself*.

Reflexive pronouns (2) G5.2

 4 Read the article and choose the correct words to fill in the gaps.

Ghostwriting

"And what do you do ¹_____?" she asked me after explaining her own work in significant detail.

"I'm a ghostwriter," I told her ²_____.

"You write about ghosts?"

"Not quite," I said ³_____ trying to stop ⁴_____ from smiling. "I write books for celebrities. Their names appear on the cover, not mine."

"What?" she said, sounding almost upset.

I prepared ⁵_____ for a series of questions.

"You mean some celebrities don't actually write their biographies ⁶_____?"

"I'm afraid so," I told ⁷_____.

The woman was Spanish so you couldn't blame ⁸_____ for not knowing what a 'ghostwriter' was. But it always surprises me that people think that someone like David Beckham sits down and writes 100,000 words about his life ⁹_____. Even if people like ¹⁰_____ had the time to write a book, they wouldn't necessarily have the talent to research and write ¹¹_____ – definitely not ¹²_____, anyway.

What people usually ask is how I satisfy ¹³_____ with doing all the work but getting none of the credit. The answer's fairly simple – it's a job. The next question comes up ¹⁴_____ within a few minutes. "So which celebrities have you written for?" Unfortunately, my contracts often state that I can never tell anyone that I wrote a book. And the book ¹⁵_____ rarely mentions me. So at this point, I hint at a few megafamous people and then change the topic of conversation.

1 a) yourselves   b) yourself   c) you
2 a) herself   b) –   c) myself
3 a) myself   b) by myself   c) –
4 a) myself   b) herself   c) me
5 a) her   b) me   c) myself
6 a) yourselves   b) ourselves   c) themselves
7 a) myself   b) her   c) herself
8 a) yourself   b) herself   c) her
9 a) himself   b) themselves   c) itself
10 a) he   b) yourselves   c) him
11 a) it   b) themselves   c) itself
12 a) themself   b) by themselves c) himself
13 a) themselves   b) me   c) myself
14 a) –   b) itself   c) it
15 a) it   b) itself   c) themselves

 5 **a)** Rewrite these sentences using the reflexive pronouns in brackets. Sometimes you will need to replace a word or add a preposition.

a) She bought the car as a 40ᵗʰ birthday present. (herself)

She bought the car for herself as a 40ᵗʰ birthday present.

b) The work is pretty boring but well paid. (itself)

_____

c) As well as me, can I ask who has also applied for the position? (myself)

_____

d) The new tax cut will benefit everyone, most of all people on low incomes like us. (ourselves)

_____

e) They need to take better care if they don't want to go down with flu again. (themselves)

_____

f) The boss of the company came in at one point to meet me. (himself)

_____

b) Match the use of the reflexive pronouns in the sentences in **5a)** to 1–3.

1 to make it clear that the object after a preposition refers to the same subject:

sentences _____ and _____ .

2 after *like*, *as well as*, *as (for)*, etc., instead of pronouns to show politeness:

sentences _____ and _____ .

3 to emphasise a noun, pronoun or noun phrase:

sentences _____ and _____ .

6 Where possible, replace an object pronoun in these sentences with a reflexive pronoun.

1 The person who did the job after me couldn't stand her either.

2 He gave the job description to her at the interview but noticed she didn't read it.

3 I asked him what motivated people like him to do such a boring job.

4 He forgot to bring his passport with him so we had to go back and get it.

5 I can't see him ever getting a place on this course, but as for you, you should think about reapplying.

5B The young ones

Verb + infinitive with *to* or verb+*ing* (1) [V5.2]

1 Complete these sentences using the correct form of the verbs in the boxes.

> ~~ask~~   let   make   agree   suggest
> promise   admit

1 JAMES   We'd like you to go on a course, Clare.
  James   *asked Clare to go on a course.*

2 MARK   Why don't you enrol on a course?
  Mark _____

3 A Let's do some more research into the matter.
  B That's a good idea.
  They _____

4 JAKE   Can I stay up to watch the film?
  DAD   No, it's time for bed.
  Dad _____

5 JANICE   It's true. I cheated in my exam.
  Janice _____

6 JO   I had to sit the exam again. The teacher said I had no choice.
  The teacher _____

7 LUCY   I won't forget again.
  Lucy _____

> allow   not mind   keep on   decide
> encourage   teach   pay

8 I gave Greg some money to help my son with his revision.
  She _____

9 A Let's go on a language course together in July.
  B OK. Let's do it!
  They _____

10 James is constantly missing classes.
   James _____

11 JON   I learned to drive with my Dad.
   Jon's dad _____

12 LINDA   Go on, Nick. Apply to university.
   Linda _____

13 ADRIAN   Doing exams doesn't worry me.
   Adrian _____

14 PAUL   The university gave me permission to reapply the next year.
   The university _____

Verb + infinitive with *to* or verb+*ing* (2) [V5.3]

2 Fill in the gaps with the correct form of the verbs in the boxes. Use an infinitive with *to* or verb+*ing*.

> go back   answer   inform   read

Regrets – I've had a few ...
I will never forget [1] _____ the first lines of that letter. "We regret to [2] _____ you that you have not passed your final examinations." It was an awful moment but I wasn't entirely surprised. In the exam, I'd forgotten [3] _____ one of the main questions. I'd meant [4] _____ when I finished. Instead, I was so relieved when I got to the end of the paper that I just didn't remember. What an idiot!

> get up   look   not take   become

I really regret [5] _____ more pictures of my kids when they were young. You think they will go on [6] _____ like the innocent little things they did when they were two. But instead, they go on [7] _____ teenagers – with absolutely none of the innocence of toddlers! And it's impossible to remember those times clearly. Mind you, I'll never forget [8] _____ at 5 a.m. every morning!

> go   say   miss   play

I truly regret [9] _____ this aloud but I was once offered the chance of a lifetime. A friend and I were invited to go for a trial at our local football club on the next Saturday. But it would have meant [10] _____ a party the night before and, being a teenager, I just couldn't do it. My parents were away and the day after the party I overslept and forgot [11] _____ to the trial. My friend went on [12] _____ football for England!

> do   go   take   be

If there's one thing I regret, it's not [13] _____ to university. I left school and went straight into work and I've been doing the same boring job for 20 years. I was always interested in politics as a teenager. Had I done a degree, maybe I would have gone on [14] _____ Prime Minister – who knows? I've always meant [15] _____ something about it – perhaps do a degree part-time. However, now it would mean [16] _____ time off work.

3 Fill in the gaps with the correct form of a verb in box A and box B.

> **A** forget (x2)   regret (x2)   mean (x2)   go on (x2)

> **B** take~~ leave   tell   move   let   apply   describe   mention

1 You never ...*forget taking*... your driving test.
2 I _____ that I would be out tonight.
3 After giving us some background, he _____ the outlook for the future.
4 I'll _____ until they give me an interview. I'm never going to give up!
5 We _____ you know last week but we couldn't get in touch with you.
6 I _____ you that I will be leaving at the end of this month.
7 The job _____ to the UK for a year.
8 Sarah _____ him now and wishes he would take her back.

4 Choose the best verb forms.

1 If you look up in that tree, you can see some birds *build/building* a nest.
2 I heard a car door *slam/slamming* shut and then the sound of raised voices.
3 I overheard them *talk/talking* in the corridor about my chances of promotion yesterday.
4 Martina could hear someone *follow/following* her, but she couldn't see who it was.
5 I saw him *drop/dropping* the empty packet on the floor.
6 We could feel the wind *get/getting* stronger as we got further from the shore.
7 I noticed someone *sit/sitting* in a car outside our house last night. I watched him *smoke/smoking* a cigarette, and then he left.

Verb-noun collocations **V5.4**

5 Choose the correct verb. Sometimes there is more than one possible answer.

1 What degree is it that he's *doing/getting*?
2 I've been *doing/getting* Spanish on and off for several years.
3 Our priority is the children *do/get* a good education.
4 To everyone's surprise, he *did/got* a place at university.
5 We've been *doing/getting* research into this for some time.
6 Having *done/got* a first in maths from Cambridge, she had the pick of several jobs.
7 He's on the verge of *doing/getting* his final exams and he's still going out every night.
8 Have you *done/got* a course in first aid yet?
9 This is the company at which I *did/got* some work experience.

6 Read the article. Fill in the gaps with a verb in the box that collocates with the underlined words/phrases.

> carried out   got   sitting
> enrolling   gain   achieving   obtain
> don't have   going on   awarded

We're used to hearing about the pressure children feel when ¹_____ important <u>exams</u> at school. However, <u>research</u> that has recently been ²_____ in the US has found children as young as 13 are getting

stressed about their future careers. These findings are further support for educationalists who argue that we are trying to make our children grow up too quickly.

"Everything in our school system is aimed at ³_____ <u>good results</u> in order to ⁴_____ either <u>a place at university</u> or a good job," says Dr Miriam Forbes, the team leader of the research. "Many children are now convinced that only people who ⁵_____ <u>a good degree</u> when they were at university, will get good jobs. Therefore, if they have little chance of going to university, they see no possibility of a successful career."

Dr Forbes thinks we already have the tools to change this situation.

"Work experience is a good example. If students ⁶_____ <u>knowledge</u> and skills about different professions while still at school, they get a greater idea of their own abilities and how they might cope in the workplace. And how even if they ⁷_____ <u>a very good education</u>, they can still enjoy and contribute to a working environment."

Meanwhile middle-class parents, especially those with money, are ⁸_____ their children <u>on more and more courses</u> – from art to zoology, believing that being ⁹_____ <u>a top degree</u> from a good university will no longer be enough. However, as Dr Forbes warns, "¹⁰_____ <u>courses</u> and other extra-curricular activities are seen as 'extra' work by this group of children. There is also some evidence that they can distract children from schoolwork while having little relevance to their future careers."

5C Priorities

Expressions connected to work V5.5

1 Fill in the gaps in these letters.

> ~~high-powered~~   self-employed
> team player   the career ladder
> against the clock   snowed under
> talking shop   taking it easy
> run-of-the-mill   pittance   fortune
> stuck in a rut   dead-end job
> deadline   take on too much work

Career quandaries

Send your career questions to us and let other readers solve them!

At university, I was always very confident about the future – I saw myself in a [1] *high-powered* job, earning a [2] _____ and [3] _____ by the time I was 45. The reality has turned out somewhat less impressive. To be honest, I'm [4] _____ . I've been in this [5] _____ for over ten years, earning a [6] _____ . The work is [7] _____ and doesn't require any brain power anymore. I fell off [8] _____ years ago! What's more, I'm so [9] _____ that I barely have time to think about a change of career.

Stephane Pendered, Liverpool

The best thing I ever did was become [10] _____ . Being your own boss means a lot more control. Sure, at times I [11] _____ – it's highly likely that you would at some point too. But working [12] _____ on a Sunday night to meet a Monday morning [13] _____ is a lot more motivating when it's your own company.
Of course, some miss working with other people. To be honest, I'd never been much of a [14] _____ . I'm terribly meticulous – some might say finicky(!) – about what I do. And the social side (or lack of it) doesn't bother me either. I used to find the constant [15] _____ down the pub after work more boring than bonding!

Dan Shavick, Cardiff

Conversational strategies RW5.1

2 Rick, Claire and Fi are having a conversation at work in the cafeteria. Fill in the gaps in their conversation.

> ~~I'd go along with that~~   Anyway, to get back to what I was saying
> What were you going to say, Claire   You've got me there
> That's exactly what I was trying to get at

RICK Sometimes I think our priorities are all wrong. We should work to live, not the other way round.

CLAIRE [1] *I'd go along with that* . But it's easier …

FI That's rubbish! I always look forward to going to work.

RICK I really wish you wouldn't butt in, Fi.
[2] _____ ?

CLAIRE I was just going to say that it's easier said than done. I mean, we've all got to go to work, haven't we?

RICK [3] _____ . I don't necessarily think we do. The main reason we all work is for money, right?

FI [4] _____ ! Anyone want another coffee?

CLAIRE No, thanks. One's enough for me.

RICK Me, too. [5] _____ , it follows that if we didn't need money, we wouldn't work – or we wouldn't work as much. So, all we need to do is 'downshift'.

> What do you mean when you say 'downshift'
> Oh, I don't know about that, Fi   Not to mention
> What I'm trying to say is   You're very quiet, Fi

CLAIRE [6] _____ ?

RICK [7] _____ that to spend less, we need to consume less. For example, smaller houses would mean smaller mortgages.

CLAIRE [8] _____ . What do you think of this 'downshifting' thing?

FI What? Sorry, I'd stopped listening. I've heard enough of Rick's ideas in the past. They're all a bit mad.

CLAIRE [9] _____ . This is the man who encouraged you to rent out a room in your house.

RICK [10] _____ how I saved you a bit when you bought your new car.

FI OK. Come on then, Rick. Tell us more about 'downshifting'.

RICK We should get back to work. How about a drink later?

● **Accurate Writing → 9, 10, 11a and 11b p85–86**

Reading and Writing Portfolio 5 p66

6 Ask the public

6A A curious science

Words with different but related meanings V6.1

1 Match the <u>underlined</u> words to meanings 1–8.

a) It's common for people to feel <u>flat</u> when returning to work after their summer holidays.

b) If you <u>break</u> it again, I won't be able to fix it.

c) I wish you'd put the <u>top</u> back on pens when you've finished using them.

d) Everyone in our house has gone down with flu but so far, I'm feeling <u>fine</u>.

e) My grandfather was a big man with <u>heavy</u> features.

f) I heard the <u>branch</u> snap and watched as it fell directly on to my car.

g) If you add two <u>odd</u> numbers together, you always get an even one.

h) The letter arrived in a <u>plain</u> brown envelope with no clues as to who it was from.

1 to cause something to separate into two or more pieces: _b)_

2 the cover or lid used to close something: ....

3 numbers such as 1, 3, 5, 7, 9, etc. : ....

4 large and strong: ....

5 not decorated or marked in any way: ....

6 not active: ....

7 healthy and well: ....

8 the part of a tree that grows out of the trunk: ....

2 **a)** Complete these sentences with the <u>underlined</u> words in **1**.

1 He keeps rather .... hours – working late into the night and then sleeping until midday.

2 Astrobiology is the .... of science that deals with the evolution of life in the universe.

3 Few people would have imagined that such a .... child would grow to be such a beautiful woman.

4 If you .... the law, be prepared to face the consequences.

5 My mother's hair is very .... , but mine is very thick.

6 Open a new bottle of lemonade – this one's gone ....

7 Max is such a .... sleeper that you literally have to shake him in the mornings.

8 By the time she was 35, she'd reached the .... of her profession.

b) Match the words you used in **2a)** to meanings 1–8.

1 not beautiful: ....

2 strange: ....

3 very thin: ....

4 disobey: ....

5 the highest part: ....

6 of a very or unusually great amount or degree: ....

7 a part of something larger: ....

8 describing fizzy drinks which are no longer fizzy: ....

Ways of comparing G6.1

3 Correct the mistakes.

1 Doing the experiment properly requires far more planning and thought that just asking a few people in the street.

2 I didn't enjoy his last film but this one is considerably better than.

3 This is easy. It isn't nowhere near as difficult as the last exercise.

4 We didn't find Sarah's presentation more impressive any than the inexperienced candidate's.

5 As the train is direct, my new journey is no longer as my old one.

6 I'm sightly better paid than I used to be but I still don't get nearly as much as I deserve.

7 You took as twice as long as Ruth did to finish the same job!

8 They're about the same age, but Sam isn't as quite confident as Isla.

9 The more scientific the research, the great the likelihood you will be taken seriously.

Formal and informal ways of comparing   G6.2

 a) Complete the article with one word/phrase in box A and one word/phrase in box B. Sometimes there is more than one possible answer.

> **A** ~~a good deal~~   pretty much
> somewhat   significantly

> **B** ~~more~~   more words
> the same   more talkative

What's in a name? Do women talk more than men? What makes people give to charity? Here's proof that not all scientific research is boring ...

The idea that women speak a [1] _a good deal more_ than men is something that about half of the population believes! But is it true? According to *The Female Mind* by Dr Luan Brizendine, women say [2] .... in a day than men – almost 20,000 for the average woman versus around 7,000 for the average man! But not everyone agrees. Deborah Cameron, an Oxford University linguistics professor, concedes that women are [3] .... than men but really, she says, the *amount* of time they spend talking is [4] ....

> **A** decidedly   distinctly more   marginally

> **B** likely   successful   more attractive

Can your name affect your life? Research by Professor Richard Wiseman on British names suggests that men called 'James' are seen as [5] .... than men called 'Ryan'. However, the situation is different when it comes to looks – with 'Ryan' at the top of the table and seen as [6] .... than 'James', which is in a close second place. Past research confirms that we do react differently to names. A study in 2002 found that certain names are [7] .... to receive better marks in class than others.

> **A** anywhere near as   good deal
> more or less   distinctly

> **B** the same   different   more likely   successful

How often do you give to charity? And what influences you to give? A study in 2007 put four different collection boxes, each representing the same charity, in bookshops around Britain. The messages on each box were [8] ....: 'Please give generously'; 'Every penny helps'; 'Every pound helps'; and 'You can make a difference'. The results, however, were [9] .... The 'Every pound helps' box was not [10] .... as the 'Every penny helps' box, which earned almost ten times as much money. Furthermore, if the box was red it was a [11] .... to get a contribution than if it was blue.

b) Complete the comments on the article using the words in brackets.

> **Ryan from Cardiff,** 2 March, 12:53
> I knew it! The reason why (half / not / I'm / brother / my / as / successful / as) [1] ....
> is just my name! It has nothing to do with the fact that (school / at / harder / miles / worked / he) [2] ....
> ...., got better results, works harder than me now and so on. It's my parents' fault!

> **Alison from Newcastle,** 3 March, 17:01
> This stuff about women talking way more than men is rubbish. (than / chattier / loads / is / boyfriend / My / am / I) [3] .... What's more, (is / near / boring / as / I'm / anywhere / not / he / as) [4] ....!

> **Dr Price from Birmingham,** 3 March, 19:57
> The reason why people often give to charity is because they don't want others to think they're tight-fisted. The reason why (than / somewhat / the / the / 'Every penny helps' / successful / slogan / more / was / others) [5] ....
> .... is obvious. (than / decidedly / the / less / alternatives / threatening / It's / message / a) [6] ....,
> making people think that any contribution is worthwhile.

But is it ethical?

Word pairs V6.2

1 Complete phrases a)–j) using *and* or *or* and a phrase in the box.

over again	miss	every	bounds	leave it
off	choose	break	tired of (sth)	parcel of (sth)

a) in leaps _____
b) each _____
c) part _____
d) hit _____
e) pick _____

f) take it _____
g) on _____
h) make _____
i) over _____
j) sick _____

2 **a)** Read the first part of an article. Fill in the gaps with phrases a)–f) from **1**.

Sponsored Links

COMPUTER SALE
Brand new laptops. Same day Delivery.
BUY NOW!
Click here for more
www.salecomputer.co.uk

CHEAP PCs UK
NOW 30% OFF
Ideal for home and business
www.cheappcsuk.com

New Laptops
Choose from a great range.
Pay less online

Banner ads are a form of advertising on the Internet. They are often small adverts running down the side of a webpage. If you click on them, you are taken to the advertiser's website.

The first banner ad appeared in 1993. Since then, this form of marketing has come on [1] _a)_ and they are now [2] _____ almost every website, commercial or otherwise. The reason is, of course, money. For [3] _____ click that is recorded on a banner ad, the owner of a website receives a small sum of money.

The success of banner ads was not instant. Back in the mid-90s, many Internet users seemed to have a [4] '_____', attitude towards this type of advertising. The subject of the adverts they saw were often somewhat [5] _____ in terms of their appeal to Internet users. Nowadays, more sophisticated technology allows banner ads to be targeted more specifically. So, if you have been searching the Internet for a new computer, you will soon find websites covered with banner ads for cheap PCs that you can [6] _____ from.

b) Read the second part of the article. Fill in the gaps with phrases g)–j) from **1**.

However, the public doesn't always react well to too much advertising, and banner ads can [7] _____ a website. For example, too many ads, or putting them in the wrong position, mean users soon become [8] _____ trying to find what they are looking for. Users then quickly learn to avoid a certain website. Google, which includes banner adverts on its search engine, have obviously got the balance right: they earn over $15 billion from them every year!

Interestingly, some website owners realised it was possible to abuse the way banner ads work. If they clicked on the ads themselves, they earned money. So, they did – [9] _____ . However, in 2004, a man was arrested for doing this and faced up to 20 years in prison for his crime.

So, are banner ads here to stay? It's not clear. Internet marketing companies seem to have an [10] _____ relationship with them – one week talking about their imminent death and the next reporting on their success. Our guess is that they'll be around for a long time yet. While everyone loves the Internet, few websites have found a way to make money other than through advertising.

Adverbs G6.3

3 Fill in the gaps with the correct adverbial form of the words in the box.

repeated	high (x 2)	scientific	ethical
late (x 2)	pretty	hard (x 2)	

1 The company comes _____ recommended. It sources all of its materials _____ and pays all of its workers a good wage.

2 The bird spread its wings _____ and then flew _____ into the air.

3 _____ , we've not been watching much television. Getting home so _____ has meant that we've been going straight to bed.

4 I'm sick and tired of _____ having to tell you to switch that thing off. You should be revising really _____ at the moment but I only ever see you playing computer games!

5 I think we need some advice. We need to investigate this problem _____ but we've _____ done any research.

Position of adverbials G6.4

 4 **a)** Match these sentence beginnings and endings from an article about advertising on TV.

1 <u>Within 10 years</u>, experts predict, ... _d)_

2 Is it because we've learned to block out ... _____

3 No – it's because technology has given us ... _____

4 The latest electrical wizardry to arrive ... _____

5 The PVR allows viewers to rewind, ... _____

6 That means that <u>every 15 minutes or so</u>, when an advert break begins, ... _____

7 <u>Alarmingly</u>, experts in the US predict that by just 2015, ... _____

a) the relentless marketing that <u>frequently</u> interrupts our favourite programme?

b) pause or fast forward through TV programmes <u>effortlessly</u>.

c) <u>in our living rooms</u> is the *personal video recorder*, or PVR.

d) advertising on TV will be dead.

e) this could be costing the advertising industry between $4 and $6 billion!

f) what is <u>possibly</u> the greatest gadget ever invented for TV viewers.

g) viewers can immediately fast forward to the next part of the programme.

b) Match each <u>underlined</u> adverbial in **4a)** to types 1–7.

Adverbial of ...

1 manner: _effortlessly_

2 indefinite frequency: _____

3 place: _____

4 level of certainty: _____

5 time: _____

6 definite frequency: _____

7 comment: _____

 5 Choose the adverbial which is in the correct position.

1 *Probably/From time to time* he has sent me flowers.

2 She *rarely/every day* watches that programme.

3 I know it's late but *here/perhaps* he's still coming.

4 When he walked into the room, the teacher didn't look at him *surprisingly/instantly*.

5 This *interestingly/definitely* looks as though it cost a lot of money.

6 *Presumably/Definitely*, he's going to meet us at the train station.

7 I watch TV *never/every so often*.

8 I read adverts in magazines *all the time/hardly ever*.

9 He's *always/as a rule* on time for appointments.

 6 Complete the sentences using the words in brackets. Sometimes there is more than one possible answer.

1 He ran _upstairs to his bedroom.._ (to his bedroom / upstairs)

2 I keep seeing his face _____ (all over the TV / lately)

3 The film ended _____ (halfway through / abruptly)

4 They work _____ (at her office / really hard)

5 We're going on holiday _____ (in the autumn / to Florida)

6 I saw that advert _____ (in England / last year)

7 He's watching TV _____ (at the moment / in his room / quietly)

8 She broke her leg _____ (in a car crash / badly / about a year ago)

7 Fill in one gap in each pair of sentences with *even* or *only*. Use the same adverb in each pair.

1 a) _____ Deb _even_ knows the answer to that question – she is so clever!

   b) _Even_ Carl _____ knows the answer to that question, so it must be easy.

2 a) _____ Dad _____ wants to help, no one else has time.

   b) _____ Mum _____ wants to help, so don't be so mean to her.

3 a) My gran is doing well with her new computer – _____ she can _____ send emails.

   b) It can't be that difficult for you to use a computer – _____ my grandfather can _____ send emails.

4 a) _____ Mark has _____ done this exercise, everyone else found it too difficult.

   b) _____ Ruth has _____ done this exercise because she didn't have time to do any more.

5 a) _____ Hugh _____ likes the smell of bacon and he's a vegetarian.

   b) She's a very unfussy baby – _____ she _____ asks for more vegetables!

Dramatic verbs V6.3

1 Read the extract from the story 'Noises in the night'. Fill in the gaps with these words/phrases.

> storming out　leapt out　grabbing　drag
> nudging　cajoling　hissed

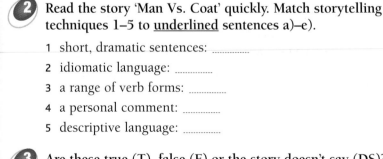

Noises in the night ...

I could feel my wife's elbow, ¹_____ me in the ribs.

"Wake up," she whispered. "I think there's someone in the house."

"What? Where?" I said sleepily, looking towards the glowing alarm clock beside my bed.

It was 3.48 a.m. I had had less than three hours' sleep, having spent between 11 and 1 ²_____ our youngest son to return to his own bed. I closed my eyes.

"Do I have to ³_____ you out of bed?" my wife ⁴_____ .

"OK! OK!" I shouted back at her and ⁵_____ of bed. "Shhhh! They'll hear you."

"Don't be ridiculous," I replied, ⁶_____ my dressing gown from the hook behind the door and ⁷_____ of our bedroom.

"There's no one in the house," I called behind me as I went down the stairs. And then I paused, "Is there ...?"

Reading

2 Read the story 'Man Vs. Coat' quickly. Match storytelling techniques 1–5 to underlined sentences a)–e).

1 short, dramatic sentences: _____
2 idiomatic language: _____
3 a range of verb forms: _____
4 a personal comment: _____
5 descriptive language: _____

3 Are these true (T), false (F) or the story doesn't say (DS)?

1 ☐ The couple met through a dating website.
2 ☐ The man was instantly attracted to the woman.
3 ☐ Before the date ended, he asked her for another date.
4 ☐ The man helped the woman with her coat.
5 ☐ He became very hot as he tried to put on his coat.
6 ☐ She thought the situation with the coat was amusing.
7 ☐ The woman left before the man could put on his coat.

● **Accurate Writing →** 12 and 13 p86

 Reading and Writing Portfolio 6 p69

Man Vs. Coat

a)THE FIRST AND ONLY TIME we met was in an upscale bar on a cold November night. I'd answered her ad in the personals column: "... would like to meet a self-assured man in his mid-thirties to early forties, a man who likes walks in the park and talks in the dark ... etc." There was a simple, lilting quality to her writing that appealed to me.

She was a tall, slender brunette in her mid-thirties. She was engaging and made good eye contact when she spoke. She was both pretty and smart, and I liked her immediately. I definitely wanted to see her again. Even better, I sensed no reluctance on her part to see me again. b)If only I could manage the rest of the evening without a *faux pas* or mishap.

As we got ready to leave, she was first to put on her heavy winter coat.

She adjusted her scarf and fitted her driving gloves to her long, elegant fingers. Once ready, she stood there, patiently waiting for me.

I lifted my parka* from the back of the bar stool and, firmly gripping the collar with my left hand, inserted my right arm into the right sleeve. With the coat half-on and half-off, I stretched my left arm to the rear in order to catch the left sleeve. But somehow my target eluded me. I tried again, and once more I missed. More determined than ever, I intensified my efforts.

Completely absorbed in what I was doing, I didn't notice that my body was beginning to twist in a counter-clockwise direction. c)As my body twisted, the coat twisted, too – the sleeve remained the same distance from my thrusting hand. I could feel beads of sweat beginning to break out on my forehead.

It was as if the sleeves had grown closer together during the last couple of hours. I grunted and groaned as I struggled to d)gain the upper hand or, more accurately perhaps, the upper sleeve. How could I have known that I was in the clutches of my own undoing? With all this twisting, my legs were beginning to corkscrew.

No man can remain upright while twisting and stabbing backward at a moving sleeve. I began to lose my balance. Slowly, I sank to the ground. Lying there in a heap with my coat partially covering me, I glanced up at my companion. e)Neither one of us said a word. Never before had she seen a man wrestled to the ground by his own coat.

MEL SINGER Denver, Colorado

*parka = a short, waterproof coat

7 Laying down the law

Language Summary 7, Student's Book p136

7A Getting away with it

Phrases with *get* V7.1

1 Match situations 1–6 with sentences a)–f).

1 A colleague asks you for some work you haven't done. ....
2 Someone asks you how your teenage children are. ....
3 A friend always criticises you. ....
4 A colleague asks how you are going to solve a problem at work. ....
5 A friend asks you about a burglary you suffered from recently. ....
6 Someone asks you about your new hobby. ....

a) I'm really getting into it, actually.
b) I can't seem to get through to them.
c) Sorry, I haven't got round to doing it yet.
d) They'll get away with it, of course.
e) Stop getting at me!
f) I've thought of a way we can get round it.

2 Fill in the gaps with the correct form of a phrase with *get*.

I had been trying to ¹ *get through to* my husband for ages about losing weight. Then, one evening, he went out and bought a new bike. He'd spent a fortune but I could finally stop ² .... him about his weight. Soon, he really ³ .... cycling and began looking much healthier. Then one Sunday, he nipped off to get a newspaper – on his bike of course. Soon, he was back – but on foot. His bike had been stolen. He'd locked it to a post but, we think, the thieves had ⁴ .... this by just lifting it off. We think we know who stole it – some local kids. But there's no proof, so they'll probably ⁵ .... it. My husband was really upset but he wouldn't do anything like trying to ⁶ .... "It's insured, isn't it?" he said. I felt sick. ⁷ .... updating the home insurance was on my 'to-do' list. But I just hadn't done it yet.

Conditionals: basic forms G7.1

3 Fill in the gaps using a zero, first, second or third conditional form of these pairs of verbs. Sometimes there is more than one possible answer.

> ~~be / get~~   lock / not be   give / get   not be / remember
> not get / not have   get / get   behave / be

1 In the UK, if you __are__ caught speeding, you __get__ a fine and three points on your licence.
2 We .... burgled if we .... to set the alarm before we went out.
3 If she .... at me so much, we .... so many rows. But she's always criticising me.
4 OK. I promise. I .... him a call tonight, if I .... round to it.
5 He's a sensible man. If he .... well in prison, he .... released in two years without a doubt.
6 If you .... your bike, it .... stolen.
7 The law in the UK says you .... a ban from driving when you .... 12 points on your driving licence.

Conditionals: non-basic forms G7.2

4 Choose the correct verb forms. Sometimes both are possible.

1 If you *might/'re going* to be away for more than a few days, you should tell your neighbour.
2 If they're coming at noon, *shouldn't/don't* we start getting ready?
3 You *give/should give* the neighbours a key if it puts your mind at rest.
4 If you *let/would let* me know about whether you can come on Saturday, it would help us in planning food.
5 If I *ever go/'m ever going* to get out of the office tonight, I'll have to miss this afternoon's meeting.
6 If you *thought/were thinking* about installing an alarm, now would be the best time.
7 We would have heard the telephone if we hadn't *rowed/been rowing*.

5 Fill in the gaps with the correct form of these verbs to make mixed conditionals.

~~not refuse~~	not worry	apply
not come	be born	have
not have	buy	not have to

1 Don't make me feel guilty about this. I _wouldn't have refused_ to help him yesterday if he weren't so arrogant.

2 If Sam .... for that job, he might be living in New York now. And we might have somewhere to stay when we go on holiday!

3 She would have the right to a US passport if she .... in the US.

4 If we .... go back and get your wallet, we wouldn't be running so late.

5 I had no phone on me or anything. If you .... home early, I would still be outside right now.

6 If you didn't butt in all the time, I .... time to explain the problems more carefully. We'll just have to hope they understood.

7 If I weren't so broke at the moment, I .... that computer we saw. It was a bargain.

8 If you had done the work when you were supposed to, you .... to stay up until midnight every night.

9 We .... about going to Florida if the weather hadn't been so terrible last time.

True stories:
My son burgled our house

As soon as I walked in I knew we'd been burgled. The police arrived within 15 minutes.

"This is strange," said one of the policemen after looking round the house. [1]" _a)_ ".

I felt sick.

I said nothing to the police but waited until my son got home.

"Was it you?" I asked him slowly.

[2] .... The moment he looked me in the eye, my suspicions were confirmed. I picked up the phone and calmly called the police.

Over the next few months, our visits with Robert in prison were emotional. He was obviously angry.

[3]" ....!" he once screamed. "What's it going to be like for me when I try and get a job in a few years' time?"

We tried to convince him that in fact the opposite was true. [4]" ...."

Now he's halfway through a two-year sentence for burglary. He's calmed down a lot now and writes to us every week. In his last letter he even said that he was glad we did what we did. [5]" ....," he wrote.

Robert now seems more convinced than us that we did the right thing. We still ask ourselves every day what we did wrong. He's an only child so we know we spoilt him a little. [6] ....

6 **a) Read the story. Fill in gaps 1–6 with sentences a)–f).**

a) Someone broke the window from ~~the inside, because there's glass outside the house~~

b) The reason why we told them was because we care about your future.

c) You didn't let me get away with it, which is possibly the reason why I'm not involved in more serious crime now.

d) You told the police because you don't love me

e) We weren't strict with him, which might be the reason why he's in prison today

f) Robert can't hide his emotions, so he couldn't get away with it

b) Rewrite the sentences in gaps 1–6 in 6a) using mixed conditionals.

1 If someone _had broken the window from the outside_ , there _would be glass inside the house._

2 If Robert were able .... , he ....

3 If you .... , you ....

4 If we didn't .... , we ....

5 If you .... , I might ....

6 If we had .... , he ....

35

7B Every step you take

Phrasal nouns V7.2

1 Make phrasal nouns from these phrasal verbs. There are three phrasal verbs that you cannot make phrasal nouns from.

1 cry out: _an outcry_
2 get together: ....
3 break in: ....
4 get at: ....
5 back up: ....
6 mix up: ....
7 set back: ....
8 look out: ....
   or ....
9 kick off: ....
10 break up: ....
11 go around: ....
12 chat up: ....
13 set on: ....
14 come in: ....

2 Fill in the gaps with the correct form of a phrasal noun from 1.

1 We got to the stadium ten minutes after .... because of heavy traffic.

2 I'm organising a little .... to celebrate Dan's birthday and wondered if you'd like to come.

3 Both my ex- and I found the .... very hard at first but we know it's for the best.

4 The .... , such as Mike's resignation and Carol's illness, will delay the project by several months.

5 We're terribly sorry but there was a .... at our office and you were sent someone else's tickets.

6 Computer stuff is always going wrong. Have you got a .... in case something happens?

7 There have been a series of .... in this neighbourhood recently and police believe it to be the work of one gang.

8 The .... that greeted the government's proposal for higher taxes has forced it to rethink its strategy.

9 The drugs do not prevent HIV from developing into AIDS, but instead claim to delay its ....

10 The company issued a warning on Wednesday, saying that the .... for the next quarter was poor.

11 The burglars had a .... who was seen sitting in a car outside the property.

12 The government has promised extra help for elderly people on low ....

Passive forms G7.3

3 Complete sentence a) with the correct form of these verbs. Then complete sentence b) with a passive form so that it has the same meaning as a).

~~know~~ smash leave say get
arrest inform watch install

1 a) The police _know_ very little about him.
   b) Very little _is known about him_ .

2 a) In the event of a break-in, you should .... your insurance company.
   b) In the event of a break-in, your insurance company ....
   ....

3 a) I left because they were .... at me the whole time.
   b) I left because I ....
   ....

4 a) Someone must have .... the back door unlocked.
   b) The back door ....
   ....

5 a) People have .... that he's not particularly honest.
   b) It ....
   ....

6 a) The council were going to .... cameras throughout the neighbourhood, but there was a huge outcry.
   b) Cameras ....
   ....

7 a) It felt like someone was .... us the whole time.
   b) It felt like we ....

8 a) Someone had .... the window and there was glass everywhere.
   b) The window ....
   ....

9 a) The police .... him on Friday night for handling stolen goods.
   b) He ....
   ....

Impersonal report structures

4 Write these headlines as sentences using *it is* + past participle + *that* clause. Use the correct form of the underlined verb.

1 GOVERNMENT <u>EXPECTED</u> TO ANNOUNCE TAX CUT THIS WEEK

   It is expected that the government will announce a

   tax cut this week.

2 <u>SUGGESTION</u> THAT MURDER GANG-RELATED

3 SUSPECT <u>ASSUMED</u> TO HAVE FLED ABROAD

4 ID CARDS <u>PREDICTED</u> TO COST TAXPAYER BILLIONS

5 CCTV CAMERAS <u>AGREED</u> TO BE INSTALLED THROUGHOUT UNIVERSITY

6 <u>ESTIMATED</u> 350,000 PEOPLE DRIVING WITHOUT INSURANCE

7 MINISTER <u>ALLEGED</u> TO HAVE ACCEPTED PAYMENTS FROM SEVERAL LARGE OIL COMPANIES

8 PRIME MINISTER <u>EXPECTED</u> TO RESIGN IN AUTUMN

5 Rewrite each sentence starting with the words in **bold**. Use the impersonal report structure: subject + passive + infinitive with *to*.

1 People say that **he** has spent 15 years researching the book. People expect **it** to be a summer bestseller.

   He is said to have spent 15 years researching the book.

2 They have agreed **proposals** that will reduce the emission of greenhouse gases. We understand that **environmental groups** are 'very excited' about the development.

3 We believe **the suspect** to be between 18 and 25. We think **he** caught a train to London on Thursday.

4 People think **the film** is his finest work to date. People expect **it** to win 'Best Picture' at the Oscars.

5 There is a rumour that **talks** have taken place recently to sign the Brazilian midfielder to Chelsea. We expect **the club** to hold a press conference soon.

6 Complete sentence b) so that it has the same meaning as sentence a). Use between three and six words.

1 a) It seems that someone has taken my keys.

   b) *Someone seems to have taken my keys.*

2 a) We have found that the drug delays the onset of the disease by up to ten years.

   b) The drug .... the onset of the disease by up to ten years.

3 a) Mr Parks appeared not to have even been in the country at the time.

   b) It .... even been in the country at the time.

4 a) We expect a delay to your flight.

   b) There .... a delay to your flight.

5 a) In the experiment, we found no significant difference between the amount of time men and women speak.

   b) In the experiment, there .... no significant difference between the amount of time men and women speak.

6 a) The public seem to be mainly in support of CCTV.

   b) It .... mainly in support of CCTV.

7 a) We think there are fewer than 1,000 pandas in the wild.

   b) There .... fewer than 1,000 pandas in the wild.

8 a) It is alleged that there are over 500,000 illegal immigrants in Britain.

   b) .... to be over 500,000 illegal immigrants in Britain.

9 a) Many consider ID cards an invasion of privacy.

   b) ID cards .... an invasion of privacy.

7C Not guilty!

Metaphors V7.3

 1 Complete these sentences with the correct form of words in the box.

> storm fly grill crack flood warm
> dawn freeze bright

1 After the trial, we .... with offers from newspapers to tell our story.

2 We had such a good time away that two weeks seem to have .... by.

3 It .... on me yesterday that next month I will have been working for this company for 20 years.

4 Being short-staffed over the last few months has meant several people have come close to ....

5 Neither of the boys are fools but Tom is distinctly ....

6 If you didn't .... me every time I go out, I might have been more honest with you.

7 "You always blame me!" she shouted, ... out of the room.

8 We arrived late at night so it was great to get a .... welcome from the owners of the bed and breakfast themselves.

9 Having thought no one was at home, he .... when he heard the sound of movement in the room upstairs.

Functions and intonation of questions RW7.1

2 a) Make questions with these words.

1 should / How / know / I / ?

....

2 coincidence / Isn't / a / that / ?

....

3 been / with / before / Anna / trouble / police / Hasn't / in / the / ?

....

4 over / time / could / just / go / this / one / If / we / more / ?

....

5 money, / any / do / you / You / have / to / seem / never / ?

....

6 back / he / Oh, / did / at / paid / he / last, / you / so / ?

....

7 we / him / crack / he'll / if / Do / think / you / question / ?

....

b) Fill in gaps a)–g) with the questions in **2a)**.

1 A Do you know where my wallet is?
  B **a)** .... I'm not your personal assistant!

2 A Tony and I have made up again after that argument about the £70.
  B **b)** ....

3 A Did you hear that the chairman's daughter has been promoted again?
  B **c)** .... That's another £10K pay rise.

4 A **d)** ....
  B Look. I've told you everything I know.
  A Well, let's start with the man who loaned you the money.

5 A £10 is fine, thanks Dad. Just until the weekend.
  B **e)** ....

6 A Something tells me the shop manager is involved in this robbery.
  B **f)** ....
  A I don't know, but let's bring him in and see what he says.

7 A I saw a police car outside her house yesterday.
  B **g)** ....
  A I think you're right. I seem to remember something a few years ago.

c) Match questions a)–g) you used in **2b)** to functions 1–7.

1 aggressive/defensive response to a question: ....

2 making a sarcastic comment: ....

3 a rhetorical question (expecting agreement): ....

4 giving instructions: ....

5 a rhetorical question (with a question tag): ....

6 checking information you think is right: ....

7 asking for new information: ....

d) Which question in **2b)** is said with a rising intonation?

- **Accurate Writing** → 14 and 15 p86–87

Reading and Writing Portfolio 7 p72

8 What's stopping you?

Language Summary 8, Student's Book p140

8A Finding the time

Phrases with *time* V8.1

1 a) Match sentence beginnings 1–10 to sentence endings a)–j).

1 With the new business, it's been impossible to find __*f)*__
2 I'm going to stay in the city for the ....
3 I'm not intolerant but I've got no ....
4 We're not in a rush so take your ....
5 We'll get there in plenty of ....
6 Please don't worry if you don't have any ....
7 It's only a matter of ....
8 Well, if you're going to start saving up, there's no ....
9 My daughter has been giving me a hard ....
10 If he's got ....

a) time if we take the train.
b) time getting ready.
c) time about the amount of stuff we throw away.
d) time like the present.
e) time to kill, why doesn't he tidy his bedroom?
f) ~~time to go out and do anything together.~~
g) time for people who are always moaning about their problems.
h) time before car journeys will become a luxury.
i) time being.
j) time to spare.

b) Complete these conversations with sentences from **1a)**.

1 A The price of petrol is getting ridiculous, isn't it?
  B I know. ....

2 A Maybe I shouldn't go out tonight. I want to buy a car in September and I'll need about £3,000 for that.
  B .... Stay in and watch a DVD with me instead.

3 A You seem to be very organised about your recycling.
  B Yes. ....

4 A I'm a bit worried about the traffic on Saturday morning.
  B That's why I think driving would be mad.
  ....

5 A I'll try and finish this today but I'm not sure I'll manage it.
  B ....

6 A Tim's always telling me how overworked and underpaid he is.
  B I'm afraid I'm not interested. ....
  ....

7 A Weren't you thinking of moving to the countryside?
  B ....
  Otherwise, I would have to commute.

8 A Are you and Sally seeing much of each other at the moment?
  B Not really. ....
  ....

9 A Seb's completely bored and says he's got nothing to do.
  B ....

10 A What time do you want to leave?
  B ....

2 Replace the <u>underlined</u> phrases with the correct form of the phrases in the box.

> have no time for   in plenty of time   take my time
> give me a hard time   it's only a matter of time
> find time   for the time being   have time to kill

1 I <u>disapprove of</u> people who waste food.
2 This leaflet says that they can't recycle plastic containers <u>at present</u>.
3 My parents have been <u>criticising me</u> about not switching off my computer at night.
4 In the future, Professor Hawkins thinks there will be a global shortage of water. "<u>It will happen – it's just *when* it happens</u>," he says.
5 <u>I've been spending as much time as I needed</u> with this project as I didn't think it was urgent.
6 If you<u>'ve got nothing to do for a while</u>, can you sort out the recycling?
7 The trouble with being self-employed is <u>arranging time</u> to go on holiday.
8 We arrived at the airport <u>earlier than it was necessary to</u>, but there was a problem with tickets.

Wish / If only G8.1

3 Complete sentence b) so it has
a similar meaning to sentence a).
Use between two and four words,
including the word in brackets. Do
not change the word in brackets.

1 a) We would like to be able to find
more time to be 'greener' but we
can't. (could)

   b) We wish __we could find__ more
time to be 'greener'.

2 a) It's terrible news that Martin is
leaving. (wasn't)

   b) I wish _____

3 a) People didn't listen to
environmentalists 20 years ago.
(listened)

   b) If _____ to
environmentalists 20 years ago.

4 a) We weren't warned about the
price increases. (been)

   b) We wish _____
about the price increases.

5 a) He won't put his paper in a
separate bin. (would)

   b) If _____
his paper in a separate bin.

6 a) My husband would like to have
spent more time with the
children when they were
younger. (wishes)

   b) My husband _____
_____ more
time with the children when
they were younger.

7 a) It's unfortunate, but people are
so selfish. (would)

   b) If _____
less selfish.

8 a) I would like more time to spare.
(wish)

   b) I _____
more time to spare.

Past verb forms with present or future meaning G8.2

4 Complete these conversations
with the correct phrase in the
box and the correct form of
the verbs in brackets.

(leave) early and (get) to the airport in plenty of time
(be) closer to Monday than Friday
(go) away in September when the schools go back
(get) round to booking them
(make up) and (stop) behaving like children
(take) my time and (do) it properly
(take) your time and (get) here safely
(go) wherever they want to and (avoid) any blame

---

1 A Why are you leaving now? You don't have to check in until six.

   B We'd prefer _____

2 A I'll do my best to get home by six but it's going to be tight.

   B I'd rather you _____

3 A Have you got any preferences for a day to meet?

   B I'd prefer it _____

4 A Martin and Sam still aren't talking after their row.

   B It's high time they _____

5 A Have you had any thoughts about when you'd like to take a holiday this year?

   B I'd sooner we _____

6 A Do you want to choose the restaurant for your parents' anniversary?

   B I'd rather _____

7 A Shall we look at some flights to Florida tonight?

   B Yes. It's about time we _____

8 A Will you have finished the decorating by Thursday?

   B I'd sooner _____

5 Rewrite sentence b) so it has the same meaning as sentence a)
using the word/phrase in brackets.

1 a) My preference would be to leave on Friday afternoon. (rather)

   b) I _____

2 a) We really should leave. (high time)

   b) It _____

3 a) Don't tell anyone about this for the time being. (sooner)

   b) I _____

4 a) Simon ought to start looking for a new job. (about time)

   b) It _____

5 a) Our preference would be for you to start on Monday. (prefer it)

   b) We _____

8B Fear!

wherever, whoever, whatever, etc. V8.2

1 Complete these sentences with *wherever*, *whoever*, *whatever*, *however*, *whenever* or *whichever*. Sometimes there is more than one possible answer.

1 You are welcome to stay at our house .... you like.

2 .... much I feed my cat, she's always hungry.

3 .... way we go, we're still going to get stuck in some traffic.

4 They can't be far away, ... they are.

5 .... did this must be punished.

6 .... just made that noise didn't sound very friendly.

2 Rewrite sentence b) so it has the same meaning as sentence a) using *wherever*, *whoever*, *whatever*, etc.

1 a) It doesn't matter where she goes, she always ends up the centre of attention.

 b) .... , she always ends up the centre of attention.

2 a) I don't know who told you that Simon and I had split up, but they were very much mistaken.

 b) ....
was very much mistaken.

3 a) I think he's an honest person no matter what people say about him.

 b) I think ....

4 a) It doesn't matter which one you choose so take what you want.

 b) Choose ....

5 a) He always gives me a call when he's in town.

 b) He gives me a call ....
....

6 a) No matter how hard you try, you'll never pass.

 b) You'll never pass, ...
....

Word building (2): suffixes V8.3

3 a) Look at these groups of words. Write the type of word (nouns, adjectives or verbs) after each group.

1 imagine, perform, excite, recover: _verbs_

2 intense, live, popular, clear: ....

3 trauma, marvel, alarm, tradition: ....

4 absorb, attract, expect, recycle: ....

b) Change each group of words in **3a)** into these types of words using the suffixes in the boxes. Make any other necessary changes.

-tion -ment -ance -y

1 nouns: _imagination_ , ... , ... , ...

-ify (x 2) -ise -en

2 verbs: .... , ... , ... , ...

-al -ic -ous -ed

3 adjectives: .... , ... , ... , ...

-ent -able -ant -ive

4 adjectives: .... , ... , ... , ...

4 Match words from **3a)** and **3b)** to definitions a)–h). Use one word from each group 1–4 in **3a)** and **3b)**.

a) _imagination_ : the ability to think of new ideas

b) ....: a thing or person that is very surprising or causes a lot of admiration

c) ....: describing an experience that causes emotional shock and upset

d) ....: describing something, e.g. a feeling that is extreme or very strong

e) ....: describing something that can be used again

f) ....: entertain people by dancing, singing, acting or playing music

g) ....: make something easier to understand by giving more details or a simpler explanation

h) ....: think or believe something will happen or someone will arrive

a) Read the instructions and do the puzzle.

- Find nouns made from these words:
  survive, responsible, challenge
- Find adjectives made from these words:
  afford, tradition
- Find verbs made from these words:
  pure, plan, sensational
- Find adverbs made from these words:
  clear, rational

R	T	L	G	L	K	T	C	Z	H	J	E	U	Z	S
E	E	A	V	N	W	X	L	C	T	V	N	C	T	E
S	P	S	A	S	N	V	E	M	I	G	X	H	R	N
P	N	U	P	U	X	E	A	D	M	U	C	A	A	S
O	U	R	R	O	S	U	R	V	I	V	A	L	D	A
N	A	V	V	I	N	O	L	Q	B	K	P	L	I	T
S	F	I	K	B	F	S	Y	A	S	B	U	E	T	I
I	F	V	D	F	E	Y	I	I	X	D	R	N	I	O
V	O	E	A	H	V	T	J	B	E	M	I	G	O	N
E	R	D	P	S	V	I	T	N	I	Z	T	E	N	A
K	D	R	A	T	I	O	N	A	L	L	Y	D	A	L
R	A	T	I	O	N	A	L	I	S	E	I	Z	L	I
A	B	R	T	B	L	H	Q	S	M	C	H	T	L	S
J	L	R	V	P	D	K	C	L	A	R	I	F	Y	E
S	E	N	S	A	T	I	O	N	A	L	I	S	T	Y

b) Complete the sentences with words you found in 5a).

1 The world's _survival_ could depend on each of us reducing our impact on the environment.

2 With increasing prices of oil and electricity, we will _____ have to think hard about our use of fuel.

3 Climate change is surely the greatest _____ facing the world today.

4 In the past, newspapers tended to _____ environmental warnings to produce dramatic headlines. Now journalists write more _____ about the growing crisis.

5 With a growing fuel crisis, the future could see us return to more _____ ways of living, with people working closer to home.

6 Currently over one billion people have no access to a clean water supply and need to _____ water before drinking.

7 It is high time we all took _____ for our impact on this planet's natural resources.

8 Currently, hybrid cars are quite expensive but within a few years, they will have become _____ to everyone.

9 We need to _____ our shopping more carefully as we are wasting too much food.

 Fill in the gaps with the correct form of the words in brackets.

http://www.medicaladvice.net/phobias

medical advice online

What is a phobia?

A phobia is a [1] _____ (persist) fear of certain situations, activities, things or people.

This fear might be something [2] _____ (logic), such as scotophobia, which is a fear of the dark. However, it can also be something entirely irrational such as octophobia, which is the fear of the number eight.

Psychologists generally [3] _____ (class) phobias into two main groups:

- Simple phobias involve a fear of specific things and the most common are, [4] _____ (predict): spiders, flying, dentists and [5] _____ (ill).

- Complex phobias include agoraphobia, which is a fear of public or unfamiliar places, and also social phobias. Both types involve a fear of [6] _____ (embarrass) or [7] _____ (humiliate) in social settings. For example, a common social phobia is glossophobia which is a [8] _____ (perform) anxiety, frequently felt by professional [9] _____ (speak) and [10] _____ (experience) actors.

What can be done about phobias?

While most simple phobias will not affect your daily life, social phobias can create extreme [11] _____ (disable). And although about one in ten people have a significant phobia, few people seek [12] _____ (treat) for it.

With professional help, however, the majority of phobia patients can beat their fears. [13] _____ (effect) relief can usually be gained from either cognitive behaviour therapy which involves talking about and rationalising your fear, medication or a [14] _____ (combine) of both.

8C The pros and cons

Reading

1 Read the poem and match questions 1–3 to speakers a)–c).

1 Who is speaking? ....
2 Who is she speaking to? ....
3 Who is she speaking about? ....

a) a new girlfriend
b) an ex-boyfriend
c) an ex-girlfriend

2 Read the poem again. Find words 1–7 and match them to meanings a)–g).

1 muted ....
2 bland ....
3 wit ....
4 flatter ....
5 vapid ....
6 wince ....
7 mince ....

a) without intelligence or imagination
b) make someone look more attractive than usual
c) describing food which has no taste
d) feel and show pain briefly and suddenly in the face
e) the ability to use words in a clever and funny way
f) meat which has been cut up into very small pieces
g) describing a colour which isn't bright

3 Tick (✓) the criticisms that the ex-girlfriend makes about the new girlfriend. Add line numbers when relevant.

a) She has poor taste. ✗
b) She isn't good-looking. ✓ *lines 9–11*
c) She is mean. ....
d) She hasn't got a very good sense of humour. ....
e) She wears high-heeled shoes. ....
f) She doesn't dress very well. ....
g) She isn't very charming. ....
h) She has an irritating voice. ....

- **Accurate Writing →** 16 and 17 p87

 Reading and Writing Portfolio 8 p75

1   You ask what I think of your new acquisition;
     and since we are now to be "friends",
     I'll strive to the full to cement my position
     with honesty. Dear – it depends.

5   It depends upon taste, which must not be disputed;
     for which of us *does* understand
     why some like their furnishings pallid and muted,
     their cookery wholesome, but bland?

9   There isn't a *law* that a face should have features,
     it's just that they generally *do*;
     God couldn't give colour to *all* of his creatures,
     and only gave wit to a few;

13   I'm sure she has qualities, much underrated,
     that compensate amply for this,
     along with a charm that is so understated
     it's easy for people to miss.

17   And if there are some who choose clothing to flatter
     what beauties they think they possess,
     when what's underneath has no shape, does it matter
     if there is no shape to the dress?

21   It's not that I think she is *boring*, precisely,
     that isn't the word I would choose;
     I know there are men who like girls who talk nicely
     and always wear sensible shoes.

25   It's not that I think she is vapid and silly;
     it's not that her voice makes me wince;
     but – chilli con carne without any chilli
     is only a plateful of mince ...

43

9 Cash

9A Where does it all go?

Price and cost V9.1

1 a) Complete these sentences with the correct form of *price* or *cost*.

a) The estimated _____ of bringing up a child from birth to 21 is over £150,000.

b) But at around £50 a head, I thought it was somewhat over-_____ .

c) However, to me it was _____less.

d) With diamonds that size, it must have _____ a fortune.

e) There are some shops which always seem to be having a half-_____ sale.

f) The insurance company didn't think it was _____-effective to repair it.

g) When I saw the _____ tag on the jacket, I thought it was a mistake.

h) The _____ of living has risen dramatically over the last few months.

i) Everything seems quite reasonably _____ , especially the main courses.

b) Fill in the gaps with sentences a)–i) from **1a)**.

1 It was an enjoyable meal, I'll admit. _____

2 _____ . The main reason has been the increase in fuel and food prices.

3 The jewellery I lost in the robbery was worth very little. _____

4 We had to get a new car after having the accident. _____

5 _____ . I often wonder how genuine these discounts are!

6 Have you read this report in the newspaper about families? _____

7 Have you seen this menu? _____

8 _____ . How can a piece of clothing cost £4,000?!

9 Did you see her ring? _____

Simple v continuous G9.1

2 a) Read the first part of the email. Fill in the gaps with the most appropriate form of the verbs in the box. Use the Present Simple, Present Continuous, Past Simple or Past Continuous.

arrive	think	email	cost	get	argue
get on	find	wait	apologise	not have	

Hi Mum, Hi Dad,

I [1] _____ from my new laptop – thanks, the best birthday present ever. We [2] _____ wi-fi in the college but yesterday I [3] _____ a café which does. I [4] _____ I'll be drinking a lot of coffee here in future!

The train eventually [5] _____ in Liverpool about an hour late – no one even [6] _____ or anything. When I got off the train, lots of people [7] _____ with some guy from the train company, "Our tickets [8] _____ a fortune," etc, etc. You can imagine the scene.

Anyway, I eventually [9] _____ to my room about eight. Carrie [10] _____ for me with a surprise birthday cake – which was really sweet of her! We have so much in common and [11] _____ really well – I'll invite her down during the next holiday.

b) Read the second part of the email. Choose the most appropriate verb form.

I've [1]*looked/been looking* at the list of books we need this term. Some of them [2]*seem/are seeming* really overpriced! However, I've also [3]*noticed/been noticing* that there's a half-price sale on at one of the bookshops at the moment. OK, so I [4]*don't do/'m not doing* an economics degree, but … I think it would be more cost-effective to buy the books now. The trouble is I've just [5]*paid/been paying* my rent and I can't really afford to. So last night I [6]*thought/was thinking* … Could I borrow the money until next term? I know you [7]*spend/'re spending* a lot of money on doing up the house at the moment so I [8]*understand/'m understanding* if it's not possible.

Anyway, I've [9]*finished/been finishing* my coffee now and I [10]*have/'m having* a lecture at 11. I'd better be off.

Hope you are both well.

Love,

Mon x

Answer Key

1A Make a good impression

1 2c) 3a) 4a) 5c) 6a) 7b) 8a) 9c) 10c) 11b) 12b)

2 2a) 've heard b) heard 3a) did
b) 've done 4a) 've made b) made
5a) 's finished b) finished

3 1 has worked 2 started 3 soon
discovered 4 has seen 5 has started
6 waited 7 did 8 has been talking
9 has been 10 asked 11 've interviewed
12 've asked

4 1a) I have finished half of my
homework so far. b) I did half of my
homework this morning. 2a) He's upset
a lot of people since he's been at the
company. b) He's made a lot of changes
since he joined the company. 3a)
During the last year, they have read
five books in English. b) During the
summer, they read two books in
English. 4a) Max has had three
interviews today. b) Amy had one
interview this morning. 5a) As soon as
he's saved up enough money, he's going
to buy a car. b) As soon as he learned
to drive, he started saving.

1B Friends – the new family?

1a) 2 on 3 out of
 b) a) b) c) phases; touch; common
   d) e) f) a regular basis; the same
   wavelength; average
   g) h) i) your depth; necessity; habit

2 2 on a regular basis 3 On average 4 out
of habit 5 on purpose 6 on the same
wavelength 7 in common 8 In phases
9 out of necessity 10 out of my depth
11 out of touch 12 in the long run

3 1 No, what happened was I left my
wallet at home and had to go back.
2 Not really, no. What happened was
I had a late lunch because I was in a
meeting most of the day. 3 No, what
happened was he tried to chat up my
friend in a bar but she was already
seeing someone. 4 Not really. What
happens is we go through periods of
chatting daily by email and then life
gets busy again. 5 What happens is we
get on well for a few weeks and then we
always fall out about something silly.

4 1 What I did was tell him a secret.
2 The person I get on best with is my
aunt. 3 Something I'd like you to do is
call me as soon as you get home.

4 The thing that annoyed me is that she
didn't call. 5 Their constant bickering is
(the reason) why they are splitting up.
6 The reason (why) those cars went out
of fashion is because they were
environmentally unfriendly. 7 What I
did was I got in touch with all his
friends. 8 This house is where we grew
up. 9 What happens is she witters on
until I stop listening.

5 2 it's the men who/that gossip more in
our office. 3 it's her constant wittering
that gets on my nerves. 4 it was only by
overhearing them that I knew about the
problem. 5 it was him that/who ended
the relationship. 6 it wasn't until you told
me that I realised how upset she was.

6a) a) It **is** normally my sisters who I talk
to about anything serious. b) Then,
what my brother does is **go** upstairs
and watch television. c) What I really
respect about **them** is that they are
supportive in everything I do.
d) It's **them** that matter to me most.
e) **What** happens is we get on well for
about two days. f) It's this year **that** is
going to be the biggest challenge.

 b) 2b) 3f) 4d) 5c) 6a)

1C Favourite sayings

1a) 1 Nothing ventured, nothing gained.
2 Once bitten, twice shy.
3 One man's meat is another man's
poison. 4 Rome wasn't built in a day.
5 Actions speak louder than words.
6 Don't make a mountain out of a
molehill. 7 Better late than never.
8 Engage mouth before brain.

 b) 2 don't make a mountain out of a
molehill. 3 engage mouth before brain.
4 Rome wasn't built in a day. 5 actions
speak louder than words. 6 nothing
ventured, nothing gained. 7 one man's
meat is another man's poison.

2 1 What I'm trying to say 2 Which isn't
to say 3 In other words 4 what this
means is 5 put it another 6 put it
simply 7 Which basically means that
8 What I mean by that 9 Which is to

2A Exceptional people

1 1 utterly 2 extremely 3 really 4 slightly
5 absolutely 6 utterly 7 rather 8 totally

2 1b) 2c) 3b) 4c) 5a) 6b) 7b)

3 1 really enjoys 2 completely agrees
3 deeply regrets 4 distinctly remembers
5 firmly believes

4 2 Colonel Michael Cobb's PhD, which he
began in 1978, is called *The Railways of
Great Britain: A Historical Atlas.*
3 The examiner who marked Michael's
thesis said, "It is a remarkable piece of
scholarship." 4 The ceremony, which is
being held in Cambridge, will be
attended by 40 members of Michael's
family. 5 Michael got his first degree at
Cambridge at Magdalene College, where
he studied mechanical sciences in the
1930s. 6 The Reverend Edgar Dowse,
who received his PhD from Brunel
University in 2004, aged 93, is the oldest
person in the world to receive one.

5a) 2 whom I have great admiration.
3 whom I complained was very tall.
4 which he never came back. 5 which
I invested went bust. 6 which the film
Twenty-One was based. 7 whom the
Nobel Prize is named.

 b) 2 My first teacher, Mr Turner, is someone
(who/that) I have great admiration for.
3 The person (who/that) I complained to
was very tall. 4 He set off on a mission
(which/that) he never came back from.
5 The business (which/that) I invested in
went bust. 6 This is the book
(which/that) the film *Twenty-One* was
based on. 7 Dynamite was discovered by
Alfred Nobel, who the Nobel Prize is
named after.

6 2 to whom I owe my life 3 with whom
I was in correspondence 4 on which he
died 5 with whom he always
collaborated 6 to which her life was
dedicated 7 in which we are standing
8 about whom millions are protesting

7 1 one; whom 2 both; which
3 none; whom 4 neither; which
5 all; which 6 most; whom

2B Memorable places

1 **What do you think about it?**
phenomenal; frustrating; tiring **How
big is it?** gigantic; minuscule; immense
How old is it? middle-aged; ancient;
elderly **What colour is it?** turquoise;
beige; pinkish **Where is it from?**
Northern European; West African;
Mediterranean **What is it made of?**
fur; polyester; stainless steel

2 2 a tiny, stunning Atlantic island
3 an inspiring, modern glass building
4 a peaceful, medium-sized medieval
town 5 a huge, brownish tropical fish
6 an inoffensive, Victorian, beige colour
7 an attractive, greyish, stone material

i

Answer Key

3 2 a breathtaking, early painting, which was signed and dated by Picasso 3 a massive, old Italian sculpture in metal and wood 4 a miserable, tiny, one-bedroomed flat which was built in the 70s 5 a long, black wool coat with white buttons

4 1 I was a little **worried** about calling her so late. 2 Can you listen for one minute without **butting** in? 3 I found the level of security **on entering** the building quite worrying. 4 The prize, **established** according to the wishes in Alfred Nobel's will, is awarded every year. 5 Passengers **leaving** on the 7.30 flight should be ready for embarkation at 7.00. 6 I can't help **gossiping** when I get bored at work.

5 2 Because 3 After 4 When 5 so 6 so 7 If 8 While 9 so 10 Because

6 b) Faced with a night sleeping in the car, we started the long journey home. c) Having rung numerous other places, and even a campsite, we were feeling more stressed than when we had left. d) Thinking about that weekend, even months later, we still fail to see the funny side. e) Bickering for over an hour, we didn't notice how low we were on petrol. f) Agreeing a short break was a good idea, we packed a small suitcase and set off on Saturday morning. g) Looking at it from the outside, the house looked fine. h) Overhearing them swap plans, I couldn't help feeling a little envious. i) Dressed entirely in black, the owner of the hotel didn't look the friendliest of hosts. j) Not having thought that hotels would be full, we hadn't bothered to book anywhere.

7 2h) 3f) 4j) 5c) 6g) 7i) 8b) 9e) 10d)

8 1 Having spent 2 played 3 Flicking 4 Needing 5 Served 6 Having woken up 7 Having lost 8 Looked after

9 2 he was knocked down by a car 3 we saw the street soon become flooded 4 Jenny's arrogance became deeply frustrating 5 I felt unappreciated by Michael

2C Spoilt for choice

1 b) medieval c) unique d) unspoilt e) golden f) diverse g) cosmopolitan

2 1a) 2d) 3f) 4c) 5e) 6g) 7b)

3 1 DS 2 F 3 T 4 DS 5 F 6 T

3A Being confident

1 **Across**
1 courageous 4 determined 5 trusting 7 meticulous 8 confident
Down
1 cautious 2 generous 3 spontaneous 6 thrifty

2 2 obstinate 3 gullible 4 extravagant 5 timid 6 finicky 7 impetuous 8 arrogant 9 tight-fisted

3 2 obstinate – determined 3 gullible – trusting 4 extravagant – generous 5 timid – cautious 6 finicky – meticulous 7 impetuous – spontaneous 8 arrogant – confident 9 tight-fisted – thrifty

4 1 It was very fortunate that they weren't fired. 2 It's pointless grumbling to your boss. 3 It is imperative that the meetings are arranged this week. 4 It can be difficult working with someone so demanding. 5 It was wholly arrogant to assume he would be safe alone in the house. 6 It is astounding that only a few weeks ago she had no experience.

5a) 2 it surprised me to see her get out 3 it wasn't a situation that continued for long 4 It frightened everyone to see him lose his temper 5 it emerged that he was going through a messy divorce 6 It's not something I'd ever want to experience

b) 8 resented it when she was offered the job 9 don't find it difficult to understand at all 10 found it funny to ask people the time 11 couldn't bear it when I came into the office after the weekend 12 preferred it when the office was more boring

3B A happy, healthy life

1 1 I got stung by a wasp on my arm and it started to **swell up**. 2 ✓ 3 He's got some kind of food poisoning – he must have picked **it up** on holiday. 4 Helen picked up a cold a few weeks ago and she still hasn't **got over it** yet. 5 ✓ 6 ✓ 7 She came out **in** a rash after eating some shellfish.

2 1 getting over 2 going around 3 picks it up 4 go down with 5 wasn't blocked up 6 Eveline had come out in spots 7 swell up 8 has put her on

3 2 Neither am I 3 Here she comes 4 have I met 5 So am I 6 she's gone down 7 There goes the man 8 It does me, too

4 **Possible answers** 1 nor can 2 I knew/had 3 Here comes/is 4 aren't I 5 so do 6 time he's

5a) a) it's a special occasion do I give in and have one. b) have restaurants started to print nutritional information on their menus. c) I've satisfied myself there are some healthy options do I decide which restaurant to go to. d) should you feel forced to have a starter and a main course. e) do I order something without asking for it to be changed in some way. f) do people eat out as healthily as they should. g) did I realise how much sugar is added to these drinks. h) will it slow you down, it will also help you enjoy your food more.

b) 1f) 2e) 3b) 4c) 5g) 6h) 7d) 8a)

6 1 Nowhere will you find better food. 2 Not only is it greasy, it tastes of nothing. 3 Only on special occasions do we eat out. 4 Seldom do people eat as many vegetables as they should. 5 Not until we got the bill did we know how expensive it was going to be. 6 In no way could burgers be described as healthy.

3C It's the way you say it

1 2 behind the times 3 hard of hearing 4 economical with the truth 5 a bit of a handful 6 senior citizen 7 seen better days 8 challenging 9 under the weather 10 a bit on the chilly side

2a) a) I think a looser pair would suit you better. b) Frankly, it could have been a bit more detailed. c) I was planning to get an early night. d) It was a bit on the short side. e) I've seen better designs. f) I'd turn it down if I were you. g) It was sort of interesting at times. h) It could do with being a bit louder.

b) 1a) 2d) 3g) 4h) 5f) 6c) 7e) 8b)

4A Society and the media

1 1c) 2b) 3c) 4c) 5a) 6c) 7b) 8c) 9b) 10a) 11b) 12a) 13a) 14c)

2 1a); b) In a), the speaker is talking about a future arrangement. In b), the speaker is talking about someone's personal plan or intention. 2a) 3a); c) In a), the speaker is talking about a personal plan or intention. In c), the speaker is talking about a decision made at the time of speaking. 4a) 5a); c) In a), the speaker is making a prediction based on opinion. In b), the speaker is talking about something that won't be completed by a certain time in the future. 6b); c) In b), the speaker is talking about a decision made at the time of speaking. In c), the speaker is talking about a personal plan or intention. 7a)

3 2✓ 4✓ 6✓ 7✓

4 2 Inflation is to go beyond 4% soon. 3 The energy price rise is due to the 'arrogance of ministers'. 4 The libel action was/has been successful – thousands are set to benefit by more than £500. 5 The minister accepts/has accepted an apology from the newspaper. 6 The England manager is due to issue a press release. 7 The government is on the verge of crisis talks.

5 1 brink of 2 sure 3 is bound to 4 likely to 5 are certain 6 are to hold 7 is set 8 ordering

6 2 We're unlikely to finish before July. 3 They're about to publish a new edition. 4 He's bound to be late. 5 Their new album is certain to be a success. 6 We're due to land at 5.30. 7 Her business is on the verge of going bust.

7 2 is set to grow; are sure to take 3 is on the verge of quitting; is likely to face 4 is on the verge of completing; is sure to include 5 is due to take place; is unlikely to be

8 1 The actor **is set** ... 2✓ 3✓ 4 The stories **are** likely to ... 5 The amount, **due to** be announced ... 6✓ 7 I definitely won't have finished it by the time he's **arrived**. 8 The new stadium will have been **built** by 2011.

4B Cities and technology

1a) 2 people 3 concept 4 former 5 rising 6 focused

  b) 2 consumers 3 idea 4 ex- 5 on the increase 6 concentrating

2 b) yet; so far c) ways; methods d) sure; convinced e) especially; particularly f) bill; demand for payment g) figures; numbers h) handsets; phones

3 1b) 2a) 3a) 4b) 5b) 6b)

4 1 were supposed to be 2 were about to have 3 weren't we going to be 4 would be needed 5 was to see 6 wouldn't have 7 would pass

5 2 Were you about to say 3 were supposed to finish 4 were to discover 5 was supposed to be delivered 6 was going to drive 7 was about to tell 8 wouldn't get 9 was to speak 10 were going to turn

6 2 We were supposed to meet at one o'clock but she didn't turn up. 3 I was going to leave early and get the four o'clock train. 4 Weren't you supposed to be working at home today? 5 The train was about to leave when we arrived. 6 We were going to make our final decision that evening.

4C Making a splash

1 2A 3B 4B 5B 6A 7A 8A 9B 10A

2 2 posted – put 3 footage – vid/video/clip 4 condemned – slammed 5 mindless and arrogant – reckless 6 unidentified – mysterious 7 riding down – roaring down 8 removed from – get off

3 1 weaving in and out 2 speed freak 3 screams past 4 way 5 mind-blowing

4 1A 2B 3 both 4A 5 both

5A Behind the glamour

1 1b) counter-attack
2a) semi-detached
b) semi-darkness
3a) overhead
b) overrated
4a) supercomputers
b) supersweet
5a) underground
b) understaffed
6a) interlocking
b) interaction

2 b) understaffed c) semi-detached d) overrated e) counter-attack f) supercomputers g) interlocking h) supersweet i) overhead j) semi-darkness k) interaction l) underground

3 1 myself/by myself 2 each other 3 it/itself 4 her/her; herself/herself 5 yourselves 6 each other 7 me 8 ourselves 9 me 10 yourself

4 1b) 2b) 3c) 4a) 5c) 6c) 7b) 8c) 9a) 10c) 11a) 12b) 13c) 14a) 15b)

5a) b) The work itself is pretty boring but well paid. c) As well as myself, can I ask who has also applied for the position? d) The new tax cut will benefit everyone, most of all people on low incomes like ourselves. e) They need to take better care of themselves if they don't want to go down with flu again. f) The boss of the company himself came in at one point to meet me.

  b) 1a); e) 2c); d) 3b); f)

6 3 I asked him what motivated people like **himself** ... 5 ... but as for **yourself** ...

5B The young ones

1 2 suggested enrolling on a course. 3 agreed to do some more research into the matter. 4 didn't let Jake stay up to watch the film. 5 admitted cheating in the exam. 6 made Jo sit the exam again. 7 promised not to forget again. 8 paid Greg to help her son with his revision. 9 decided to go on a language course together in July. 10 keeps on missing classes. 11 taught him to drive. 12 encouraged Nick to apply to university. 13 doesn't mind doing exams. 14 allowed Paul to reapply the next year.

2 1 reading 2 inform 3 to answer 4 to go back 5 not taking 6 looking 7 to become 8 getting up 9 saying 10 missing 11 to go 12 to play 13 going 14 to be 15 to do 16 taking

3 2 forgot to mention 3 went on to describe 4 go on applying 5 meant to let 6 regret to tell 7 means moving 8 regrets leaving

4 1 building 2 slam 3 talking 4 following 5 drop 6 getting 7 sitting; smoke

5 1 doing/getting 2 doing 3 get 4 got 5 doing 6 got 7 doing 8 done 9 did/got

6 1 sitting 2 carried out 3 achieving 4 obtain 5 got 6 gain 7 don't have 8 enrolling 9 awarded 10 Going on

5C Priorities

1 2 fortune 3 taking it easy 4 stuck in a rut 5 dead-end job 6 pittance 7 run-of-the-mill 8 the career ladder 9 snowed under 10 self-employed 11 take on too much work 12 against the clock 13 deadline 14 team player 15 talking shop

2 2 What were you going to say, Claire? 3 That's exactly what I was trying to get at 4 You've got me there 5 Anyway, to get back to what I was saying 6 What do you mean when you say 'downshift' 7 What I'm trying to say is 8 You're very quiet, Fi 9 Oh, I don't know about that, Fi 10 Not to mention

6A A curious science

1 2c) 3g) 4e) 5h) 6a) 7d) 8f)

2a) 1 odd 2 branch 3 plain 4 break 5 fine 6 flat 7 heavy 8 top

  b) 1 plain 2 odd 3 fine 4 break 5 top 6 heavy 7 branch 8 flat

3 1 Doing the experiment properly requires far more planning and thought **than** just asking a few people in the street. 2 I didn't enjoy his last film but this one is considerably better ~~than~~. 3 This is easy. It isn't **anywhere** near as difficult as the last exercise. 4 We didn't find Sarah's presentation **any more** impressive than the inexperienced candidate's. 5 As the train is direct, my new journey is no longer **than** my old one. 6 I'm **slightly** better paid than I

Answer Key

used to be but I still don't get nearly as much as I deserve. **7** You took **as** twice as long as Ruth did to finish the same job! **8** They're about the same age, but Sam isn't **quite as** confident as Isla. **9** The more scientific the research, the **greater** the likelihood you will be taken seriously.

4a) 2 significantly more words **3** somewhat more talkative **4** pretty much the same **5** distinctly more successful **6** marginally more attractive **7** decidedly likely **8** more or less the same **9** distinctly different **10** anywhere near as successful **11** good deal more likely

b) 1 I'm not half as successful as my brother **2** he worked miles harder at school **3** My boyfriend is loads chattier than I am **4** I'm not anywhere near as boring as he is **5** the 'Every penny helps' slogan was somewhat more successful than the others **6** It's a decidedly less threatening message than the alternatives

6B But is it ethical?

1 a) and bounds b) and every c) and parcel of (sth) d) and miss e) and choose f) or leave it g) and off h) or break i) and over again j) and tired of (sth)

2a) 2c) **3**b) **4**f) **5**d) **6**e)

b) 7h) **8**j) **9**i) **10**g)

3 1 highly; ethically **2** prettily; high **3** Lately; late **4** repeatedly; hard **5** scientifically; hardly

4a) 2a) **3**f) **4**c) **5**b) **6**g) **7**e)

b) 2 frequently **3** in our living rooms **4** possibly **5** Within 10 years **6** every 15 minutes or so **7** Alarmingly

5 2 rarely **3** perhaps **4** instantly **5** definitely **6** Presumably **7** every so often **8** all the time **9** always

6 2 all over the TV lately/lately all over the TV. **3** abruptly halfway through. **4** really hard at her office. **5** in the autumn to Florida/to Florida in the autumn. **6** in England last year/last year in England. **7** quietly in his room at the moment. **8** badly in a car crash about a year ago.

7 2a) Only Dad wants to help, no one else has time. **b)** Mum only wants to help so don't be so mean to her. **3a)** My gran is doing well with her new computer – she can even send emails. **b)** It can't be that difficult for you to use a computer – even my grandfather can send emails. **4a)** Only Mark has done this exercise, everyone else found it too

difficult. **b)** Ruth has only done this exercise because she didn't have time to do any more. **5a)** Even Hugh likes the smell of bacon and he's a vegetarian. **b)** She's a very unfussy baby – she even asks for more vegetables!

6C Short story radio

1 1 nudging **2** cajoling **3** drag **4** hissed **5** leapt out **6** grabbing **7** storming out

2 1e) **2**d) **3**a) **4**b) **5**c)

3 1F **2**T **3**DS **4**F **5**T **6**F **7**DS

7A Getting away with it

1 1c) **2**b) **3**e) **4**f) **5**d) **6**a)

2 2 getting at **3** got into **4** got round **5** get away with **6** get his own back **7** Getting round to

3 2 wouldn't have been; had remembered **3** didn't get; wouldn't have **4** 'll give; get **5** behaves; 'll be **6** had locked; wouldn't have been **7** get; get

4 1 're going **2** shouldn't **3** should give **4** let **5** 'm ever going **6** were thinking **7** been rowing

5 2 had applied **3** had been born **4** hadn't had to **5** hadn't come **6** would have had **7** would have bought **8** wouldn't have **9** wouldn't worry

6a) 2f) **3**d) **4**b) **5**c) **6**e)

b) 2 If Robert were able to hide his emotions, he could have got away with it. **3** If you loved me, you wouldn't have told the police. **4** If we didn't care about your future, we wouldn't have told them. **5** If you had let me get away with it, I might be involved in more serious crime now. **6** If we had been strict with him, he might not be in prison now.

7B Every step you take

1 2 get-together **3** break-in **5** backup **6** mix-up **7** setback **8** lookout; outlook **9** kick-off **10** break-up **13** onset **14** income

2 1 kick-off **2** get-together **3** break-up **4** setbacks **5** mix-up **6** backup **7** break-ins **8** outcry **9** onset **10** outlook **11** lookout **12** incomes

3 2a) inform **b)** should be informed **3a)** getting **b)** was being got at the whole time. **4a)** left **b)** must have been left unlocked. **5a)** said **b)** has been said that he's not particularly honest. **6a)** install **b)** were going to be installed throughout the neighbourhood (by the council), but

there was a huge outcry. **7a)** watching **b)** were being watched the whole time. **8a)** smashed **b)** had been smashed and there was glass everywhere. **9a)** arrested **b)** was arrested (by the police) on Friday night for handling stolen goods.

4 2 It is suggested that the murder is/was gang-related. **3** It is assumed that the suspect has fled abroad. **4** It is predicted that ID cards are to cost the taxpayer billions. **5** It is agreed the CCTV cameras are to be installed throughout the university. **6** It is estimated that 350,000 people are driving without insurance. **7** It is alleged that the minister has accepted payments from several large oil companies. **8** It is expected that the Prime Minister is to resign in the autumn.

5 1 He is said to have spent 15 years researching the book. It is expected to be a summer bestseller. **2** Proposals have been agreed to reduce the emission of greenhouse gases. Environmental groups are understood to be 'very excited' about the development. **3** The suspect is believed to be between 18 and 25. He is thought to have caught a train to London on Thursday. **4** The film is thought to be his finest work to date. It is expected to win 'Best Picture' at the Oscars. **5** Talks are rumoured to have taken place recently to sign the Brazilian midfielder to Chelsea. The club is expected to hold a press conference soon.

6 2 has been found to delay **3** appeared (that) Mr Parks hadn't **4** is expected to be **5** was found to be **6** seems (that) the public are **7** are thought to be **8** There are alleged **9** are considered (by many) to be

7C Not guilty!

1 1 were flooded **2** flown **3** dawned **4** cracking **5** bright **6** grill **7** storming **8** warm **9** froze

2a) 1 How should I know? **2** Isn't that a coincidence? **3** Hasn't Anna been in trouble with the police before? **4** If we could just go over this one more time? **5** You never seem to have any money, do you? **6** Oh, so he paid you back at last, did he? **7** Do you think he'll crack if we question him?

b) a)1 b)6 c)2 d)4 e)5 f)7 g)3

c) 1a) 2c) 3e) 4d) 5b) 6g) 7f)

d) g)

8A Finding the time

1a) 2i) 3g) 4b) 5a) 6j) 7h) 8d) 9c) 10e)

b) 1 It's only a matter of time before car journeys will become a luxury. 2 Well, if you're going to start saving up, there's no time like the present. 3 My daughter has been giving me a hard time about the amount of stuff we throw away. 4 We'll get there in plenty of time if we take the train. 5 Please don't worry if you don't have any time to spare. 6 I'm not intolerant but I've got no time for people who are always moaning about their problems. 7 I'm going to stay in the city for the time being. 8 With the new business, it's been impossible to find time to go out and do anything together. 9 If he's got time to kill, why doesn't he tidy his bedroom? 10 We're not in a rush so take your time getting ready.

2 1 have no time for 2 for the time being 3 giving me a hard time 4 It's only a matter of time 5 've been taking my time 6 've got time to kill 7 finding time 8 in plenty of time

3 2 Martin wasn't leaving. 3 only people had listened/listened 4 we had been warned 5 only he would put 6 wishes he had spent 7 only people would be 8 wish I had

4 1 to leave early and get to the airport in plenty of time. 2 took your time and got here safely. 3 was closer to Monday than Friday. 4 made up and stopped behaving like children. 5 went away in September when the schools go back. 6 go wherever they want to and avoid any blame. 7 got round to booking them. 8 take my time and do it properly.

5 1 would rather leave on Friday afternoon. 2 is high time we left. 3 would sooner not tell anyone about this for the time being. 4 is about time Simon started looking for a new job. 5 would prefer it if you started on Monday.

8B Fear!

1 1 whenever 2 However 3 Whichever 4 whoever; wherever 5 Whoever 6 Whoever; Whatever

2 1 Wherever she goes 2 Whoever told you that Simon and I had split up 3 he's an honest person whatever people say about him 4 whichever one you want 5 whenever he's in town. 6 however much you try.

3a) 2 adjectives 3 nouns 4 verbs

b) 1 imagination, performance, excitement, recovery 2 intensify, liven, popularise, clarify 3 traumatic, marvellous, alarmed, traditional 4 absorbent, attractive, expectant, recyclable

4 b) marvel c) traumatic d) intense e) recyclable f) perform g) clarify h) expect

5a)

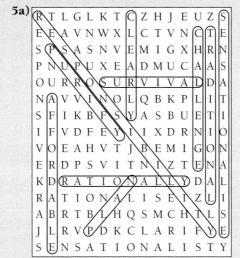

b) 2 clearly 3 challenge 4 sensationalise; rationally 5 traditional 6 purify 7 responsibility 8 affordable 9 plan

6 1 persistent 2 logical 3 class/classify 4 predictably 5 illness/illnesses 6 embarrassment 7 humiliation 8 performance 9 speakers 10 experienced 11 disability/disabilities 12 treatment 13 Effective 14 combination

8C The pros and cons

1 1c) 2b) 3a)

2 1g) 2c) 3e) 4b) 5a) 6d) 7f)

3 c) ✗ d) ✓ line 12 e) ✗ f) ✓ lines 20 and 24 g) ✓ lines 15–16 h) ✗

9A Where does it all go?

1a) a) cost b) priced c) price d) cost e) price f) cost g) price h) cost i) priced

b) 1b) 2h) 3c) 4f) 5e) 6a) 7i) 8g) 9d)

2a) 1 'm emailing 2 don't have 3 found 4 think 5 arrived 6 apologised 7 were arguing 8 cost 9 got 10 was waiting 11 get on

b) 1 been looking 2 seem 3 noticed 4 'm not doing 5 paid 6 was thinking 7 're spending 8 understand 9 finished 10 have

3 1 fit 2 do they weigh 3 looks 4 only have 5 is being 6 're having 7 're weighing 8 don't see 9 come 10 imagine 11 'm thinking 12 appears 13 are feeling

4 2a) looks b) are looking 3a) is having b) have 4a) comes b) is coming 5a) see b) Are you seeing 6a) Do you feel b) feels 7a) is appearing b) appear 8a) think b) Are you thinking 9a) weighs b) 'm weighing 10a) are fitting b) fits 11a) Did I imagine b) imagine 12a) is b) is being

9B Cash-free

1 **Across**

3 roadworthy 4 meat-free 7 like-minded 8 fashion-conscious

Down

1 washable 2 student-led 5 waterproof 6 childish

2 2 The salesperson claimed that this computer would be futureproof but I know it won't. 3 My dad won't use the Internet to buy things as he thinks it's untrustworthy. 4 It's an appealing investment as it's tax-free. 5 The company is proud that all of its products are market-led. 6 My mother has become a lot more politically-minded as she's got older. 7 He was quite tall and wearing a reddish sweater. 8 Disposable nappies create a million tonnes of waste in the UK every year.

3 1 an 2 – 3 A 4 the 5 – 6 – 7 the 8 a 9 – 10 the 11 the 12 the 13 the 14 a

4 3 I'm going out for ~~one~~ **an** hour or two. 4 It will take about **a/one** week for the money to be transferred into your account. 5 Nick said he'd come round ~~an~~ **one** evening next week. 6 Can I speak to the manager? I've been passed from ~~an~~ **one** idiot to another for the last half **an** hour. 7 He kicked **a/one** shoe off and then **the** other and put his feet on the table. 8 Have you got **one/a** 50-pence piece for this parking meter? 9 What **an** idiot I am! I've forgotten my wallet. 10 I don't know where my teenage son is from **one** day to the next. 11 This is your cake recipe, isn't it? Do you use ~~an~~ **one** egg or two? 12 My daughter is **a/one** year old on Wednesday so I'm taking ~~one~~ **a** day off. 13 I knew that ~~a~~ **one** day he would become a famous singer. 14 The oldest living person died at the age of **a/one** hundred and twenty-two!

5 1 Quite a few 2 a little 3 a few 4 little 5 Quite a few 6 a little 7 Few

6 1b) 2a) 3b) 4a) 5b) 6c) 7b) 8c) 9a) 10b) 11a) 12c) 13b) 14a) 15c) 16b)

Answer Key

9C A gloomy science?

1 1 nuclear 2 resources 3 renewable 4 overseas 5 developing 6 record 7 growth 8 production 9 market 10 decline 11 discrimination 12 superpower

2a) 1 So, to sum up 2 First of all 3 let's start by looking 4 Just to recap 5 Last but not least 6 Leaving salaries aside for a moment 7 To go back to the issue 8 I'm going to divide my talk into

b) 1f) 2b) 3e) 4d) 5c) 6a)

3 b) 4 c) 7 d) 8 e) 2, 3 f) 1, 5

10A Be creative!

1 1 is 2 are 3 contributes 4 are 5 seems 6 is 7 is 8 have 9 feels 10 indicate; is/was/has been 11 was 12 is not 13 was 14 are 15 is 16 embarrasses 17 is 18 was

2 2 the world; thinks 3 politics; appears 4 courses; appeal 5 my ideas; were ignored 6 theories; have been proposed 7 my parents; were 8 people; read

3 1 Both of my sons **have** studied English since they were at primary school. 2 ✓ 3 News reports **are** coming in of an exciting takeover bid in the world of sport. 4 ✓ 5 To attempt to learn a language without reasons **is** destined to end in failure. 6 The *Lord of the Rings* films **were** all directed by Peter Jackson. 7 ✓ 8 Gossiping with colleagues **is** always dangerous.

4 2 audience; have 3 university; is 4 team; includes 5 BBC; has/have 6 audience; is 7 public; are 8 family; are 9 Spain; is/are 10 family; lives

5 1 there's one thing that annoys me, it's people wittering on about the price of this and that for ages. 2 entirely agrees with me. 3 came out in a rash when I started taking the medicine. 4 regret not working hard at school. 5 up to my eyes in work these days. 6 warned him over and over again about gossiping. 7 getting round the (problem of the) lack of security might be to install an alarm. 8 to kill, can you sort out the recycling? 9 whatever I say. 10 costs a fortune.

6 1 have a row is she waits for me to apologise first. 2 of whom had heard anything about the problem. 3 left early, we didn't need to rush. 4 (us) hours to sort out the problem. 5 do I read a newspaper from cover to cover. 6 of resigning. 7 near as fit as I used to be. 8 to be in good health. 9 we left. 10 go by train.

10B Stick with it!

1 2 low 3 opaque 4 patterned 5 heavy 7 vague 8 modern 9 Tight 10 aggressive

2 1b) 2a) 3c) 4c) 5b) 6b) 7b) 8c) 9a) 10b) 11a) 12a)

3 1 can't 2 must 3 could 4 might 5 should 6 might 7 will 8 won't 9 would 10 may 11 must 12 'll

4 1 have told 2 be having 3 wait/be waiting 4 be thinking 5 have found 6 miss 7 have been 8 should have got

5 2 may be better by the weekend. 3 would have hated the film, so I'm glad you didn't come. 4 wouldn't have broken your computer on purpose. 5 must be enjoying themselves out in California. 6 will be waiting for you. 7 won't have been my brother you saw. 8 can't have revised enough.

10C Go for it!

1 a)

2 1c) 2d) 3a) 4f) 5b) 6e)

3 1c) 2b) 3c) 4a)

Reading and Writing Portfolio 1

1a) Possible answers a), c), d), e)

2 2c) 3e) 4d)

3 2DS 3T 4F 5F 6DS

4 However, unlike alcohol and drugs, Dr Carr believes that this communication addiction can usually be overcome by relatively simple methods.; With children, and for their parents, the situation is perhaps more worrying.; The statistical findings of the survey are telling.; Julie is not overly worried by her situation but feels she is losing touch with her sons.

5 Her latest book is entitled *Was it really any different when we were young?*; A third of parents interviewed felt the need to keep up with technology was a burden on the family budget.; Besides, mobile phones are not particularly expensive these days.

6 a)T b)F c)T d)F e)T f)F

7 1a)S b)T 2a)T b)S 3a)S b)T 4a)S b)T 5a)T b)S

8 1a) 2c) 3a)

9 1a), c) 2a), b) 3b), c)

10a)
1 Communication is central to everything we do. 2 Firstly, choose the right time and the right place. 3 Organise your ideas in your mind before attempting to communicate them. 4 Be articulate in your speaking. 5 Communication is a two-way process.

Reading and Writing Portfolio 2

1 a)3 b)2 c)4 d)1

2 1a) 2b) 3c) 4b) 5a) 6c)

3 1f) 2a) 3b) 4d) 5c) 6g) 7e)

4 defence, defense; jewellery, jewelry; metre, meter; moustache, mustache; tyre, tire

5 2 LOWER 3 BE DEFEATED 4 HAPPEN 5 SEASON

6 2 fall from grace 3 fall into someone's trap 4 nearly fall off your chair 5 fall on hard times 6 fall short

7 2 informal, b) 3 informal, a) 4 formal, d) 5 informal, f) 6 formal, e)

8 1 thought about 2 cliché 3 encouragement 4 affected 5 Whenever 6 rely on 7 talk sense 8 level-headed 9 man 10 half the woman

Reading and Writing Portfolio 3

1 d) Only two people have requested it.

2 1 To-the-Max. 2 It has no sauna.

3 1 Work Out has a swimming pool, sauna and spa facility, but To-the-Max doesn't. 2 The programmes are more varied and the gym has more group fitness studios. 3 To-the-Max. 4 A financial contribution from the company. 5 A greater range of fitness classes and more flexibility with membership.

4 a) renovate b) take up (sth) c) offset d) subsidy e) in terms of f) opt out

5a) 1 on the other hand 2 differences between 3 Although 4 key difference 5 In contrast 6 but 7 the larger 8 However 9 more 10 differ in 11 while

b) 2

c) b)2, 4 c)9 d)7 e)1, 5, 11 f)3, 8 g)6

6 2 However 3 but/while 4 differ in 5 Although 6 a more 7 however/on the other hand/in contrast 8 but/although 9 the more 10 While/Although

Reading and Writing Portfolio 4

1 1F 2T 3T 4T

2 1a) 2b) 3a) 4c) 5a) 6c)

3 2 look up to 3 captivated by 4 personality 5 insight 6 trivial 7 ability 8 thought-provoking

4a) 2c) 3f) 4b) 5g) 6d) 7a)

b) 3

5 b)2 c)1, 4, 7 d)3 e)6

Reading and Writing Portfolio 5

1 1c) 2a)

2 1T 2F 3F 4T 5F 6F 7F 8T

3 1c) 2a) 3b) 4a) 5c) 6b)

4 1B 2E 3C 4A 5D

5 1 The writer and the readers. 2 To involve the reader and give him/her a sense of being part of his story. 3 The writer and the children in the orphanage. 4 *myself*. The writer emphasises that he is referring to himself. 5 *you*. Having involved the readers, he wants to shift the focus back on to them as individuals who can act for themselves.

6 2 us 3 us 4 I 5 I 6 my 8 I 9 me 10 I 11 me 12 you 13 you 14 you 15 yourself

7 **Possible answers** 2 We sometimes feel 3 When I was young, I 4 I hated my 5 Why should I waste time doing unpaid work? 7 me 8 I met some extraordinary people 9 I know 10 you should 11 you can get involved

Reading and Writing Portfolio 6

1 1B 2A 3C 4A, C 5B

2 **background** B has seen an advertisement in the *Guardian*. C have a nine-month contract to rent a house – there are problems promised to be resolved before moving in
problem A the Internet connection speed is always less than 2MB/s C a leak in the roof, carpet that needed cleaning and a faulty freezer
effect A the Internet connection is useless in the evening B customers are misled C nothing has been done
solution A contact to advise when/how problem will be resolved B investigation of the advertisement C resolve the problems within two weeks
warning A matter will be passed to solicitor

3 a)7 b)5, 4 c)2 d)6 e)1 f)3

4 A switch off/switch on B look forward (to) C moving in

5 1c) 2e) 3a) 4d) 5f) 6b)

6 2 **inventing** problems 3 **review** your records 4 **wait** any longer 5 **respected** your company 6 **resolving** this problem 7 **arrived** an hour late 8 **continue** sending

7 **Possible answers** 1 three friends and I 2 enclose 3 minutes 4 arrived 5 I was told 6 annoyed 7 cancelled 8 left 9 ~~You ruined our evening – thanks a lot!~~ 10 ~~I apologise for writing this letter of complaint, but~~ 11 disappointed 12 I would appreciate it if I could receive an explanation. 13 ~~And you should expect to hear from my solicitor.~~ 15 Yours faithfully,

Reading and Writing Portfolio 7

1 a)

2a) 1b) hardworking 2a) drowns b) unknown c) all levels of Venetian society 3a) gripping b) a convincing c) well-written 4a) a great crime story b) doesn't need c) recommends

b) 1 Introduction and background 2 Story 3 Evaluation 4 Recommendation

3a) a) exasperating b) sumptuous c) subtle d) satisfying e) multifaceted f) lucid g) dedicated h) must-read

b) 1 sumptuous 2 subtle, lucid, satisfying, must-read 3 exasperated, dedicated, multifaceted

c) 1 satisfying 2 multifaceted 3 sumptuous 4 lucid

4a) *The Girl of His Dreams* 2, 3, 4, 9, 13, 14, 15 **Donna Leon** 6 **Brunetti** 11, 12 **the writing** 8

b) 4

5 2 It 3 It 4 mystery/novel 5 she 6 her 7 Her 8 his 9 he 10 policeman 11 his 12 novel/mystery

6 2 It 3 tale/story 4 Leon 5 her 6 she 7 policeman 8 he 9 his 10 story/tale 11 the writer's 12 she

Reading and Writing Portfolio 8

1a) 3

b) 2

c) 3

2 b) New c) Zealand d) Queenstown e) bungy f) jump g) jumped h) terrified i) guide j) platform k) breathe l) falling m) slow n) motion o) pulled p) flying

3 2 stuff 3 freak out 4 full-on 5 sweet 6 cool

4a) b)3 c)2 d)1 e)5

b) 2d) 3c) 4e) 5b)

5 b)

6 2 sweet 3 full-on 4 stuff 5 freaked out 6 cool

7 b) Up until that point, everything is sweet. c) … the waiver forms and stuff. d) Like, this was 43 metres down … e) I still don't know why or how, but I JUMPED! f) Everything in slow motion … g) It's not OK, it's not OK! No way is it OK! h) But really scary! i) … the water's coming closer and closer … j) And I was thinking …

8 2 coolest 3 full-on 4 What a thrill! 5 Well 6 SO AMAZING 7 But 8 freaked out 9 stuff like that 10 there's this huge, dark shape that's passing by 11 awesome

Reading and Writing Portfolio 9

1 2d) 3e) 4b) 5f) 6c)

2 1c) 2b) 3b) 4c) 5b) 6d)

3a) 2e) 3a) 4d) 5f) 6c)

b) b) reason and result c) addition d) condition e) time f) purpose g) comment adverbial

4 1c) 2f) 3e) 4d) 5a) 6b)

5a) **Possible answers** 2 Why are Oyster cards such a good idea? 3 What should I do if I lose my card? 4 When I get my card, what should I do first? 5 What is the most important thing to remember about Oyster cards? 6 Do I have to be from the UK to buy a card?

b) b) As a result of Oyster cards, the transport network has become virtually cashless c) Not only is it more convenient, but you will save money too. d) Provided e) From then on, f) so that g) In fact,

6a) 2d), g) 3b), e) 4c), f)

Reading and Writing Portfolio 10

1 b)2 c)5 d)4 e)1

2 a) protruded b) broad c) lean d) screen door e) haze f) hover g) listless h) fan i) windshield

Answer Key

3 Possible answers 1 It is a remote place that receives few visitors. **2** Yes, because he doesn't seem to be in a hurry. **3** She seems used to the boredom and loneliness of her job. **4** It is American slang for being drunk. **5** "I <u>seen</u> him about three months ago. He had a operation. <u>Cut somepin</u> out." (I saw him about three months ago. He had an operation. They cut something out.); "<u>Doesn't</u> seem no longer than a week I <u>seen</u> him myself. <u>Looked</u> fine then. He's a nice sort of a guy when he <u>ain't stinko</u>." (It doesn't seem longer than a week since I saw him myself. He looked fine then. He's a nice sort of guy when he isn't drunk.) **6** It means that no-one is allowed to ride on the truck other than the driver. **7** Because he thinks it will be impossible to ask for a ride. **8** He is young, but looks much older. He seems to have had a hard life, and done a lot of hard manual work.

5a) 2 red/shining red **3** lean, lonely **4** little, screened **5** quiet **6** dark brown **7** high, wide **8** broad

b) 1 excitedly **2** silently **3** slowly

c) 1 buzzed, butting **2** spurted

6 1 roared **2** rocketing **3** blazed **4** weeping **5** peering

7 2 pigs **3** a small child **4** a rock **5** a baby's **6** a sheet **7** ice

8 Possible answers 1 There was a sudden noise as the door opened and the young woman strode aggressively into the room. She was tall and had elegant clothes. Her face was as cold as ice. **2** An old man stood silently in front of the abandoned house. He was smoking heavily. Every so often he would look up sadly at the window of the house. **3** "You going to tell her?" she asked him softly. "Might do," he snapped angrily. "It depends." **4** The doorbell rang loudly. He jumped up, walked quickly to the door and opened it. A small boy was standing frightened in front of him.

Accurate Writing

1 1 not only **2** as well/too **3** also **4** as well/too **5** Besides **6** Also/What's more

2 1 I don't know if **they're** at home at the moment. **2 Who's** coming to your party tomorrow? **3** We would have helped you if we could **have**. **4** You're going to be late for **your** meeting if you don't leave soon. **5** I would have been here earlier but **there** weren't any trains. **6** I think that's their car but I don't know **whose** bike that is.

3 1 Ever since **2** While/As **3** first/originally **4** the moment/as soon as **5** Ever since/From then on **6** Meanwhile

4 1 It's highly unlikely **we'll** be there on time. **2** Someone left this coat at my **son's** party. Is it **yours**? **3** We aren't exactly sure of **its** age but my **husband's** friend thinks **it's** about 200 years old. **4** My **parents** are in their 70s but **they're** very active. **5** The **town's** unspoilt character makes it a lovely place to visit. **6** That **one's** mine, your **ones** are still in the fridge.

5 1 However/But **2** whereas **3** but/although **4** Even though/Although **5** even though

6 1 may be **2** everyday **3** two metres **4** anyone **5** every one **6** any way

7 2 nonetheless, a) **3** However,/Nevertheless, e) **4** However,/Nevertheless, c) **5** although d)

8 Newspapers in the UK are commonly split into broadsheets and tabloids. The most popular broadsheet, which is published Monday to Friday, is the *Daily Telegraph*. It's owned by brothers David and Frederick Barclay, who live on the tiny island of Brecqhou in the English Channel. The most popular daily tabloid is the *Sun* and is owned by Rupert Murdoch, the Australian media mogul, who also owns *The Times* and the TV station Sky.

9 2 Lately, we've been seeing a lot of each other. **3** Prior to joining this company, I was earning a pittance. **4** Subsequent to our conversation yesterday, we would like to make a formal offer of employment. **5** Up until a month ago I was unemployed.

10 1 She told me the news **straightaway**. **2 Lately**, she's been really fed up with work. **3** She'd **finally** decided it was time to move on. **4** I **instantly** knew she was making a mistake. **5** And before **giving in** her resignation, I pleaded with her to listen to me. **6 An hour later**, I had convinced her to think a little harder. **7** And **at the end of the day**, over coffee, she agreed to think on her decision for another week.

11a) 1 science **2** sufficient **3** either **4** achieve **5** neighbour **6** conceited **7** shriek **8** piece **9** ceiling **10** foreign

b) either, achieve, conceited, shriek, piece, ceiling

12 2 She got dressed in the dark so as not to disturb her sister. **3** We worked late in order that we avoided working at the weekend. **4** Please provide us with a daytime telephone number in order for us to contact you quickly. **5** They spoke quietly so no-one would overhear them.

13 2a) colon **b)** semi-colon **3a)** semi-colon **b)** colon **4a)** semi-colon **b)** colon **5a)** colon **b)** semi-colon

14 1 Supposing; As long as **2** whether/if; otherwise **3** Imagine; unless **4** If; Assuming/Provided

15 1 Despite the enormous outcry, plans for the new airport are proceeding. **2** Incredibly, they got away with the robbery. **3** "I can't get through to him," she said desperately. **4** I travelled to Italy, Spain, France and Turkey last year. **5** My eldest brother, who lives abroad, is a rich, successful businessman. **6** The wallpaper, which was a disgusting mix of brown, yellow and green, was peeling off the walls. **7** The address is 120 Hills Road, Newtown, Hampshire.

16 1 Quite honestly,/Frankly, **2** Surely/Obviously, **3** Apparently, **4** Fortunately, **5** Amazingly, **6** Frankly, **7** Surely **8** According to

17 1 receipts **2** government **3** exaggerated **4** accommodation **5** admitted **6** colleagues

18 1 Due/Owing **2** Due to/As a result of **3** Because of/Owing to **4** As/Since **5** consequently/therefore **6** Because of/Due to

19a) -ible visible, credible, eligible **-able** portable, valuable, memorable, laughable

b) b) memorable **c)** portable **d)** eligible **e)** visible **f)** laughable **g)** valuable **h)** credible

Simple v continuous: verbs with different meanings G9.2

 3 Choose the best verb form.

ATTENDANT   This bag won't ¹*fit/be fitting* in the overhead lockers, I'm afraid. You'll have to put it in the hold.

MAN   OK, I'll just take out my laptop first.

ATTENDANT   Are these all your bags?

MAN   Yes. How much ²*are they weighing/ do they weigh*?

ATTENDANT   I'm afraid it ³*looks/is looking* as though you might be significantly above your weight allowance which means you'll have to pay an extra fee.

MAN   But we ⁴*only have/are only having* four bags!

ATTENDANT   It's not the amount, sir. It's the weight. The airline ⁵*is/is being* quite strict about this at the moment. We ⁶*have/'re having* a lot of trouble with people taking too much luggage on flights back from the US because of the weak dollar.

JO   What's happening, Dad?

MAN   They ⁷*weigh/'re weighing* our luggage.

ATTENDANT   With the extra bag that has to go in the hold, you're 25 kilos above your allowance. So that's … $500.

MAN   What? That's a fortune!

ATTENDANT   It's $20 per kilo.

MAN   That's ridiculous. I ⁸*don't see/'m not seeing* why it's so expensive.

ATTENDANT   These are safety rules that ⁹*come/ are coming* from the aviation authority, not from the airline, sir.

MAN   I ¹⁰*imagine/'m imagining* the prices are set by you, though.

ATTENDANT   How would you like to pay?

MAN   At these prices I ¹¹*think/'m thinking* of leaving some stuff behind.

ATTENDANT   Well, that's up to you, sir.

WOMAN   What's wrong, dear?

MAN   We've got to pay for excess baggage.

WOMAN   How much is it?

MAN   Well, it ¹²*appears/'s appearing* to be more expensive than the flight itself.

JO   Dad. Can you buy me a drink?

WOMAN   Not now, Jo. Your dad and I ¹³*feel/ are feeling* a little poor at the moment.

 4 Complete each pair of sentences with the same verb. Use the Present Simple in one sentence and the Present Continuous in the other.

~~expect~~	look	imagine	have	see
come	be	think	fit	weigh	feel	appear

1 a) We __expect__ him to arrive soon.
   b) Is that the door bell? Are you __expecting__ anyone?

2 a) This house actually _____ reasonably priced.
   b) We _____ at houses all weekend so we can't come over.

3 a) She _____ some last-minute doubts about whether to take this job or not.
   b) Do you _____ time for a quick cup of tea?

4 a) The wood for all the garden furniture we sell _____ from sustainable forests.
   b) Our new car _____ on Sunday. I can't wait!

5 a) I don't entirely agree with you but I _____ your point.
   b) _____ you _____ anyone at the moment?

6 a) _____ you _____ alright? You look very pale.
   b) I hate this phone. It _____ so plasticky.

7 a) Next year my friend _____ in a film with Christian Bale. It's her biggest role to date.
   b) Can you lend me £20? I _____ to have left my wallet at home.

8 a) We _____ his painting work is reasonably priced but we won't be using him again.
   b) _____ you _____ of investing any of your inheritance?

9 a) This bag _____ a lot! Can you help me?
   b) A What are you doing?
      B I _____ some flour. I need 400 grammes.

10 a) Our neighbours _____ solar panels on their roof, which will save them a fortune in fuel bills.
    b) One of the problems of losing all this weight is that nothing _____ me any more.

11 a) _____ I _____ it, or did there used to be a cashpoint here?
    b) I _____ the shops will be really busy because of the sales.

12 a) This exercise _____ really tough.
    b) Our two-year-old _____ really difficult at the moment, but I guess it's what we should expect.

Word building (3): productive suffixes V9.2

1 Complete the puzzle with words using these suffixes.

-led	-free	-worthy	-minded
-able	-proof	-ish	-conscious

Across (→)

3 A car that isn't suitable to be driven on the road isn't … (10)

4 Vegetarians eat food that is … (4–4)

7 Two people that think in a similar way are … (4–6)

8 Someone who cares a lot about what they wear is … (7–9)

Down (↓)

1 Something that can be washed is … (8)

2 A class activity that is controlled by students is … (7–3)

5 Something that does not allow liquids to pass through it is … (10)

6 Someone that behaves immaturely is … (8)

 2 Rewrite these sentences using the suffixes in brackets. Make any other necessary changes.

1 We've become a lot more aware of security since we were burgled. (-conscious)

  We've become a lot more security-conscious since we
  were burgled.

2 The salesperson claimed that this computer would not become obsolete in the future but I know it will. (-proof)

3 My dad won't use the Internet to buy things as he thinks you can't trust it. (-worthy)

4 It's an appealing investment as you don't have to pay tax on it. (-free)

5 The company is proud that all of its products are initiated by the market. (-led)

6 My mother has become a lot more aware of politics as she's got older. (-minded)

7 He was quite tall and wearing a sort of red sweater. (-ish)

8 Nappies that you can dispose of create a million tonnes of waste in the UK every year. (-able)

a/an, the or no article G9.3

3 Read the blog. Fill in the gaps with *a*, *an*, *the* or no article (–).

Buy Nothing Day

Cash-free … for a day!

'Buy Nothing Day' is [1]_____ informal day of protest which began in [2]_____ Canada in 1992. [3]_____ young artist called Ted Dave was getting fed up with the high prices of things and [4]_____ amount we all buy – especially at [5]_____ Christmas. So, for just one day every year, he decided he would buy nothing.

Ted's argument was that we have got so used to spending [6]_____ money that we have stopped thinking about it. And in doing so, we waste [7]_____ world's resources. Consumerism has become [8]_____ significant part of our culture and 'Buy Nothing Day' reminds us that there is more to life than [9]_____ shopping.

Now people in over 65 countries from Madrid to Mumbai participate in [10]_____ protest. It happens on [11]_____ last Friday in November, which is one of [12]_____ busiest shopping days in [13]_____ US.

Of course, 'Buy Nothing Day' isn't just about changing your lifestyle for just one day. Organisers want it to be [14]_____ lasting relationship with your consumer conscience. And remember, they say, it's free!

a/an v one; few, a few, quite a few [G9.4]

 4 Change the <u>underlined</u> word(s) in each sentence to *a/an* or *one*, where appropriate. If more than one answer is correct, give the alternatives.

1 I've only got <u>a</u> *one* credit card, whereas my wife's got five.
2 If you can hold on <u>one</u> minute, I'll come with you. *or a*
3 I'm going out for <u>one</u> hour or two.
4 It will take about <u>a</u> week for the money to be transferred into your account.
5 Nick said he'd come round <u>an</u> evening next week.
6 Can I speak to the manager? I've been passed from <u>an</u> idiot to another for the last half <u>an</u> hour.
7 He kicked <u>a</u> shoe off and then <u>the</u> other and put his feet on the table.
8 Have you got <u>one</u> 50-pence piece for this parking meter?
9 What <u>an</u> idiot I am! I've forgotten my wallet.
10 I don't know where my teenage son is from <u>one</u> day to the next.
11 This is your cake recipe, isn't it? Do you use <u>an</u> egg or two?
12 My daughter is <u>a</u> year old on Wednesday so I'm taking <u>one</u> day off.
13 I knew that <u>a</u> day he would become a famous singer.
14 The oldest living person died at the age of <u>a</u> hundred and twenty-two!

 5 Complete these sentences with *few, a few, little, a little*, or *quite a few*.

1 A lot of people I know have little credit card debt. _____ of them – almost all, in fact – pay off their credit cards in full every month.
2 I have _____ time on Wednesday if you would like me to help.
3 I've only got _____ passwords for websites as I can't remember too many.
4 I have _____ time for people who borrow too much money and have trouble paying it back. It's their own fault!
5 _____ times last year – almost every month in fact – I thought our business was going to go bankrupt.
6 I've saved _____ money over the past few years but nowhere near enough for a deposit on a house.
7 _____ people would say they don't ever worry about money.

 6 Read the article. Choose the correct word/phrase for each gap.

How much cash do you carry?

I usually have ¹ _____ emergency ten-pound note tucked at the back of my wallet but otherwise I carry ² _____ cash. I carry ³ _____ coins as I hate the weight of money in my pockets. Plus they make ⁴ _____ annoying sound when I walk. I always carry ⁵ _____ credit card wherever I go.

1	a) a	b) an	c) a few	
2	a) very little	b) few	c) a little	
3	a) a few	b) few	c) little	
4	a) an	b) one	c) a	
5	a) a little	b) a	c) a few	

⁶ _____ people I know never seem to have any money on them. I don't know whether this is practical or they are just being tight-fisted! Personally, I wouldn't feel comfortable if I didn't have at least ⁷ _____ cash on me. In reality, there are ⁸ _____ times you'll find me with less than $100 in my purse. I think it comes from ⁹ _____ evening when, needing ¹⁰ _____ taxi home, I went to ¹¹ _____ ATM and it was broken. I had to walk home and I was terrified. I swore it would never happen again!

6	a) Few	b) One	c) A few	
7	a) little	b) a little	c) quite a few	
8	a) quite a few	b) little	c) few	
9	a) one	b) a	c) the	
10	a) one	b) a	c) –	
11	a) an	b) a	c) one	

Virtually none. I rely on plastic the whole time. I've got ¹² _____ credit cards – about eight – which means that I'm never worried if ¹³ _____ of them doesn't work for some reason. Sometimes I find it difficult to buy small things – like ¹⁴ _____ newspaper – but ¹⁵ _____ day I think you'll be able to pay for everything with ¹⁶ _____ credit card.

12	a) few	b) a few	c) quite a few
13	a) few	b) one	c) a few
14	a) a	b) one	c) little
15	a) a	b) –	c) one
16	a) one	b) a	c) little

9C A gloomy science?

News and economics V9.3

1 Do the puzzle.

```
¹N       R
 ²R E     S
³R   W   E
⁴O   S  S

    ⁵D   E       G
     ⁶R  C   D
      ⁷G  O   H
         N
       ⁸P  O     N
        ⁹M   T
¹⁰D    I  E
  ¹¹D    C        N
    ¹²S       R
```

a) The first ¹_____ power plant was opened in Russia in 1954.

b) The diminishing supply of the earth's natural ²_____ and the instability in the regions that provide them, are causing increased interest in ³_____ energy sources such as solar and wind energy.

c) Although ⁴_____ aid to ⁵_____ countries now totals over $100 billion per year, it is falling in real terms.

d) Despite ⁶_____ levels of economic ⁷_____ in the last decade in China, which has averaged at over 10%, the World Bank estimates that 35% of the country lives on under $2 a day.

e) Mass ⁸_____ has existed since the 16ᵗʰ century in Italy where the largest shipyard employed 16,000 people and produced nearly one ship every day.

f) The health of the housing ⁹_____ is seen as one of the key indicators as to the state of a country's economy.

g) The longest period of economic ¹⁰_____ – known as the Great Depression – was in the 1920s and 1930s.

h) Before legislation against gender ¹¹_____ adverts for the same job commonly displayed one salary for men and a lower salary for women.

i) In the 21ˢᵗ century, we can expect countries such as China, India and Russia to join the US and gain economic ¹²_____ status.

Presenting information RW9.1

2 a) Complete these extracts from a presentation about gender discrimination using the words in brackets.

a) ¹_____ , (So / up / sum / to) we've come a long way in 50 years but we're not there yet.

b) ²_____ , (all / First / of) ³_____ (by / start / looking / let's) at some past examples of gender discrimination. Thirty years ago, it was common for men and women to receive different wages for the same job.

c) ⁴_____ , (to / Just / recap) we've so far looked at the situation in both the past and the present – and found that although some things have changed, discrimination is alive and well in our workplaces. ⁵_____ , (least / Last / but / not) what about the future?

d) ⁶_____ , (a / for / aside / salaries / Leaving / moment) discrimination is also evident when it comes to promotional opportunities. That is, men are more likely to get promoted than women.

e) ⁷_____ (the / issue / to / back / go / To) of women being paid less than men, you may think this no longer happens. In fact, it does – and there is currently no law that can simply prevent employers from carrying out this practice.

f) ⁸_____ , (to / my / into / going / divide / talk / I'm) three different sections: the past, the present and the future.

b) In which order do you think extracts a)–f) appeared in the presentation?

1 _____   3 _____   5 _____

2 _____   4 _____   6 _____

3 Match phrases 1–8 in 2a) to functions a)–f).

a) Signalling a new point: __6__

b) Summarising what's been said so far: _____

c) Referring to a point made earlier: _____

d) Telling the audience what we are going to speak about: _____

e) Making the first point: _____ , _____

f) Signalling the last point: _____ , _____

• **Accurate Writing → 18, 19a) and 19b) p87**

Reading and Writing Portfolio 9 p78

10 The key to success

10A Be creative!

Subject/verb agreement G10.1

1 Complete these sentences with the correct form of the verb in brackets.

1 Serious illness .... (be) rare in my family.

2 Congratulations .... (be) in order for everyone who passed their exams.

3 The United States .... (contribute) the largest amount of overseas aid in the world but the least amount per person.

4 Fifty states .... (be) voting on the same day in the forthcoming US election.

5 The news at the moment .... (seem) to be full of economic doom and gloom.

6 Whoever stole the paintings .... (be) likely to have had some inside help.

7 Overseas .... (be) where my father spent most of his childhood.

8 The earth's resources .... (have) been under threat for thousands of years.

9 Two hours in a car .... (feel) like a long time to a two-year-old.

10 Statistics .... (indicate) this May .... (be) the wettest since records began.

11 Whoever gave you that information .... (be) lying.

12 £200,000 .... (not be) much money in the housing market these days.

13 When I was at school, maths .... (be) my worst subject.

14 Marathons .... (be) typically 42.195 kilometres in length.

15 She enjoys all aspects of maths but statistics .... (be) her main passion.

16 Having rows in public with my boyfriend .... (embarrass) me.

17 Diabetes .... (be) a syndrome which results in abnormally high blood-sugar levels.

18 They gave me $50 for the chairs, which .... (be) a lot of money in those days.

2 Complete the sentences with a word/phrase in box A and the correct form of a verb in box B.

> **A** ~~my class~~   people   my ideas   courses
>   the world   politics   my parents   theories

> **B** ~~is/are~~   has been proposed/have been proposed
>   read/reads   was/were   think/thinks   appear/appears
>   was ignored/were ignored   appeal/appeals

1 Everyone in ___my class___ ___is___ better at languages than I am!

2 I don't know anyone in .... who .... that economics is an interesting subject!

3 With your interest in current affairs, I would have thought something like .... on your shortlist for a degree.

4 I haven't made a final decision yet but a couple of .... particularly .... to me.

5 Although all of .... at the meeting, I'm not going to give up.

6 A number of .... to explain exactly how we learn languages but none of them are conclusive.

7 Both of .... good at maths but I've always found it quite tough.

8 Plenty of .... still .... newspapers, but the industry is still in decline.

3 Tick (✓) the correct sentences. Then correct the mistakes.

1 Both of my sons has studied English since they were at primary school.

2 For a banker, his politics are surprisingly left-wing.

3 News reports is coming in of an exciting takeover bid in the world of sport.

4 I haven't met anyone who hasn't at some point wanted to be famous.

5 To attempt to learn a language without reasons are destined to end in failure.

6 The *Lord of the Rings* films was all directed by Peter Jackson.

7 What we found inspiring was his talk on creativity.

8 Gossiping with colleagues are always dangerous.

4 Fill in the gaps with a noun in the box and the correct form of the verb in brackets. Use the Present Simple. If both singular and plural verb forms are possible, give both.

~~Chelsea Football Club~~   family (x 2)   Spain
public   audience (x 2)   university   team   BBC

1 _Chelsea Football Club_ _regret/regrets_ (regret) to announce the resignation of their manager and head coach.

2 The _____ _____ (have) taken their seats and the performance is expected to begin in a few minutes.

3 I don't believe this. This _____ _____ (be) offering a degree in 'Creativity'.

4 The celebrity basketball _____ _____ (include) film stars, musicians and even a couple of politicians.

5 The _____ _____ (have) announced plans to launch a channel dedicated to sport.

6 The _____ for the opening ceremony of the Olympics _____ (be) reported to have reached two billion.

7 The _____ _____ (be) voting on Tuesday in all 50 states and within a week, we may be witnessing political history.

8 My _____ _____ (be) flying in from all over the world to come to my wedding.

9 _____ _____ (be) beating England at the moment. They have just scored a brilliant goal.

10 His _____ _____ (live) abroad so he doesn't see them very often.

Review: vocabulary

 5 Rewrite these sentences using the correct form of a word/phrase in the box.

entirely agree   my eyes   cost a fortune
get round   regret   witter on   over and over again
come out   whatever   kill

1 a) If there's one thing that annoys me, it's people talking about the price of this and that for ages.

   b) If _____

2 a) He feels the same way as I do.

   b) He _____

3 a) A rash appeared when I started taking the medicine.

   b) I _____

4 a) I wish I'd worked hard at school.

   b) I _____

5 a) I'm incredibly busy with work these days.

   b) I'm _____

6 a) I've repeatedly warned him about gossiping.

   b) I've _____

7 a) One way of avoiding the problem of the lack of security might be to install an alarm.

   b) One way of _____

8 a) If you've got nothing to do for a while, can you sort out the recycling?

   b) If you've got time _____
   _____

9 a) He won't listen no matter what I say.

   b) He won't listen, _____

10 a) Every year, our holiday is very expensive.

   b) Every year, our holiday _____

Review: grammar

6 Complete b) so it has the same meaning as a).

1 a) If we have a row, she waits for me to apologise first.

   b) What she does if we _____
   _____

2 a) I spoke to two people at the company. They both had heard nothing about the problem.

   b) I spoke to two people at the company, neither _____

3 a) We left early so we didn't need to rush.

   b) Having _____

4 a) We spent hours sorting out the problem.

   b) It took _____

5 a) I hardly ever read a newspaper from cover to cover.

   b) Rarely _____

6 a) He will resign very soon.

   b) He is on the verge _____

7 a) I used to be a lot fitter.

   b) I'm not anywhere _____

8 a) The doctors said it appears he is in good health.

   b) The doctors said he appears _____
   _____

9 a) We really should leave.

   b) It's high time _____

10 a) Going by train is my preference.

   b) I'd sooner _____

10B Stick with it!

Antonyms V10.1

1 Complete each sentence with the correct word from each pair of adjectives.

> nasty/~~sour~~   dark/heavy
> patterned/rich   opaque/rough   low/short

1 A These cherries are a bit __sour__, aren't they?

  B Yes, that tree has never produced any sweet ones. I don't know why.

2 A Which building is your office? The tall one with the mirrored windows?

  B No, that's some Japanese bank. I work in the _____ building next to it.

3 A I like the bathroom in that house. It's really bright.

  B Yes, although it would be better if the glass in the window were a bit more _____ . At the moment, everyone can see you inside from the street!

4 A I'm looking for a plain black skirt for work.

  B We've got this one – which is very subtly _____ . What do you think?

5 A I thought I'd make you something light as I knew you'd get in late.

  B Thanks. I had a _____ lunch with some clients so that's perfect.

> ~~sweet~~/wet   aggressive/strong
> weak/faint   difficult/tight   young/modern

6 A Did you ask for a dry wine?

  B Yes, but this is quite __sweet__ isn't it?

7 A I've made the coffee quite strong. Is that OK?

  B Perfect. One thing I really can't stand is _____ coffee.

8 A Their house looks very old from the outside.

  B Yes, but the design inside is _____ .

9 A I think I'm going to take these back. I wanted easy-fit jeans.

  B Oh, sorry. What did I get you?

  A _____-fit. I look like a 1980s rock star!

10 A Thomas used to be such a gentle little boy.

  B I know. Now he can be so _____ at times.

  A I guess it's just being a teenager.

Modal verbs (1): functions G10.2

2 Read the article. Choose the most appropriate verb for each gap.

The secrets of my success

We asked six business leaders for their most important piece of advice on getting to the top of their profession.

> Be grateful. You ¹ _____ always thank people for their help – however small it is. I ² _____ always prioritise someone's request who I know is grateful for my help.

> I ³ _____ allow my day to get hijacked. The only way I ⁴ _____ to do everything I need to in the morning is by switching off my email until, say, lunchtime.

> Avoid criticism. Telling people what they ⁵ _____ have done is rarely constructive. Everyone ⁶ _____ have their own method of doing things and some are, inevitably, better than others.

> You ⁷ _____ treat everyone equally – regardless of their position. Just because someone has less status in a company than you doesn't mean you ⁸ _____ be rude to them.

> Sometimes you ⁹ _____ to worry. Predicting what ¹⁰ _____ go wrong in projects will save you from future headaches.

> You ¹¹ _____ stay organised – especially if you have a lot to remember. You ¹² _____ rely on your brain, either. Make lists, write plans, whatever.

1 a) could	b) should	c) need
2 a) will	b) would	c) have to
3 a) don't manage to	b) shouldn't	c) won't
4 a) allow	b) can	c) manage
5 a) need	b) should	c) must
6 a) could	b) is allowed to	c) manages to
7 a) may	b) must	c) ought to have
8 a) will	b) would	c) can
9 a) need	b) must	c) allowed
10 a) is able to	b) could	c) should
11 a) have got to	b) must	c) have to
12 a) can't	b) couldn't	c) may not

Modal verbs (2): levels of certainty about the past, present and future G10.3

3 Complete the conversations with the modal verbs in the boxes. Use each modal verb only once.

| could | can't | must | might |

CLIVE I really don't know how she affords all those clothes.

KAREN I know. She ¹ .... be earning much more than us.

CLIVE She ² .... have some other source of income. There's no other explanation. What ³ .... it be?

KAREN For all we know, she ⁴ .... have won the lottery.

| might | will | should | won't |

MUM I'm starting to get anxious about Sam. He ⁵ .... have arrived by now. He ⁶ .... have had an accident.

DAD You know Sam. He ⁷ .... have left late and have about three other things to do on the way. He ⁸ .... be long.

| may | must | 'll | would |

OLLIE Your parents don't mind looking after Sally at the weekend, do they?

ANNA Of course not. They ⁹ .... have said something otherwise.

OLLIE I ¹⁰ .... give them a quick call. Just to check. What do you think?

ANNA If you ¹¹ .... call them, do it tomorrow. They ¹² .... be watching a film now. They always do on Saturday nights.

4 Complete these sentences with the correct form of the verb in brackets.

1 I may .... (tell) you this last week. I can't remember.

2 We shouldn't go round until a bit later. They might .... (have) dinner.

3 I may not .... (wait) outside when you get here. It looks as though it's about to rain.

4 Did you see that pile of property details? They must .... (think) of moving.

5 I'm so pleased you accepted the job. I know you must .... (find) it a difficult decision to leave your previous company.

6 It's high time I went home. I'll .... (miss) the last train otherwise.

7 I tripped over your bag on the stairs again last night. I'm OK but it could .... (be) a nasty accident.

8 If there were no delays at the airport, he should .... (get) home last night.

5 Rewrite these sentences using the correct form of the modal verb in brackets.

1 It was definitely difficult for him. (would)
   It would have been difficult for him.

2 It's possible that the weather will be better by the weekend. (may)
   The weather ....

3 It was the kind of film you hate, so I'm glad you didn't come. (would)
   You ....

4 I really don't think he broke your computer on purpose. (wouldn't)
   He ....

5 I'm absolutely certain that they are enjoying themselves out in California. (must)
   They ....

6 Call him. He's bound to be waiting for you. (will)
   Call him. He ....

7 I'm sure that the person you saw wasn't my brother. (won't)
   It ....

8 I'm convinced she didn't revise enough. (can't)
   She ....

10C Go for it!

Reading

 1 **What is the cartoon's main message?**

a) Consumerism will never make you happy.
b) Whatever you do, you'll never be happy.
c) If you keep working hard, you will eventually be happy.

2 **Read the article. Fill in gaps 1–6 with sentences a)–f).**

a) Layard worries that societies, and in particular governments, have got it all wrong.
b) He argues convincingly that we can quite accurately measure the happiness of an individual.
c) At first it felt like we were living in a mansion.
d) That is, the more we get, the more we want – and therefore the more money we need.
e) The impressive thing about Layard's book, however, is how clearly and concisely he speaks to an average reader.
f) Inflation and unemployment are low, yet people report that they are less happy.

 3 **Read the article again. Choose the best answers.**

1 Once you have the basic necessities of life, scientists have found …
   a) you become less happy when you earn more money.
   b) you need a lot more money to make you happier.
   c) earning more money does not always make you happier.
2 Layard thinks that positive economic growth …
   a) is not an accurate measure of a country's economic status.
   b) does not fully represent what society wants.
   c) makes us feel unhappier.
3 Layard wants …
   a) to establish an official measure of society's happiness.
   b) people to stop buying things to make themselves happy.
   c) people to stop being obsessed with money.
4 Layard's ideas …
   a) are not all his own.
   b) are confusing to someone without some knowledge of economics.
   c) have already helped several governments around the world.

 Reading and Writing Portfolio 10 p81

The science of happiness

Some time around our daughter's first birthday, we moved out of our Central London flat and into the suburbs. ¹____ . *We* had a bedroom, *our daughter* had a bedroom, *I* had an office, and we *still* had a spare bedroom for guests! I was so happy.

The feeling didn't last.

Soon I started looking at the larger houses at the top of our road. I started grumbling to my wife, regretting why we hadn't just borrowed more money and gone for somewhere bigger. I was unhappy again.

Apparently I was suffering from 'the hedonic treadmill' – a theory that states that we adapt to any improvement in our lives, but then soon look for more. ²____ . Well, that all makes sense, doesn't it? After all, we all know that the more money you have, the happier you are. Right?

Wrong.

According to scientists, if you have very little, some money *does* make you happier. However, once you have a home, food and clothes, happiness fails to rise significantly with increased income. And this is a subject which of late seems to be fascinating economists, including Richard Layard, author of *Happiness: Lessons from a New Science*.

³____ . They regard economic growth as the most significant measure of a country's success. Layard, on the other hand, reminds us that, as Aristotle said over 2,000 years ago, what we in fact pursue is happiness.

During the past 50 years, Layard points out, consumerism has become the most important thing in society; we live in better houses, drive better cars, eat tastier food and go on more exotic holidays than we did half a century ago. ⁴____ .

The reason is that one's happiness is somewhat more complex than the state of one's bank balance. Layard identifies seven factors that influence people's happiness: family relationships, financial security, work, community and friends, health, personal freedom and personal values. ⁵____ . And that this measurement better represents the success of a society than traditional measures of economic growth.

The theories here are far from new and several countries already attempt to measure the happiness of their people. They even state that it is part of their government's aim to increase the happiness of their voters – and their wealth, of course! ⁶____ . I have no diploma in economics, yet I was (almost) never lost in this fascinating book.

Reading and Writing Portfolio 1

Topic sentences

Reading an article about a modern problem
Writing topic and supporting sentences
Review communicating

 a) Read the first paragraph of the article on page 55. Which of these ideas would you expect to read about?

a) How to treat addiction to communication.
b) How to write shorter emails.
c) The signs of addiction to communication.
d) A psychologist's view of the problem.
e) Why you shouldn't let your children have mobile phones.

b) Read the complete article and check your answers.

 Read the article again and fill in gaps 1–4 with one of these sentences. There are two extra sentences.

a) ~~A recent survey reveals an emerging downside of the technological revolution in communication.~~
b) So far, the problem is restricted to a very small number of people.
c) Computer Addiction Services in Washington runs treatment programmes for people addicted to technology.
d) Dr Seb Carr, the director of an addiction clinic in Los Angeles, frequently sees these worrying signs in his patients.
e) Do any of these 'warning signs' sound familiar?
f) We don't often consider the amount of electricity used by computers.

 Are these sentences true (T), false (F) or the article doesn't say (DS)?

1 [T] Dr Carr believes a communication addiction is not difficult to treat.
2 [ ] Doctors feel inadequately trained to deal with this modern problem.
3 [ ] The survey discovered that parents want to spend significantly more time with their children.
4 [ ] Julie Akehurst thinks her children need professional treatment.
5 [ ] Dr Palser believes the problem with teenagers is getting out of control.
6 [ ] Dr Palser thinks parents need to monitor what their children do on the Internet more closely.

Help with Writing Topic and supporting sentences

 The sentences in **2** are *topic sentences*. They highlight the topic of a paragraph which is supported by the other sentences in the paragraph. <u>Underline</u> the topic sentences in paragraphs E–H in the article.

 The sentences that follow or surround the topic sentence are *supporting sentences*. They develop or support a topic sentence. Find sentences in paragraphs I–K which are not a supporting sentence of the <u>underlined</u> topic sentences.

 Look at the article again. Are these sentences true (T) or false (F)?

Topic sentences:

a) [ ] help readers to understand the main content of each paragraph.
b) [ ] never appear at the beginning of a paragraph.
c) [ ] can be a question.
d) [ ] are not always complete sentences.
e) [ ] can appear in the middle of a paragraph.
f) [ ] never appear at the end of a paragraph.

7 Are these sentences topic (T) or supporting (S) sentences?

1a) [ ] The ease of email can discourage interpersonal communication.
b) [ ] The introduction of email has given us a way to deliver messages instantly and efficiently.
2a) [ ] In classes, teachers claim that mobile phones are a common source of disciplinary problems.
b) [ ] Checking and sending text messages frequently distract students from their work.
3a) [ ] If you've emailed about the same topic three times, it's time to pick up the phone and have a conversation.
b) [ ] One method for dealing with email addiction is the 'Rule of Three'.
4a) [ ] The Centre for Online Addiction claims people are lying about the time they spend online.
b) [ ] Internet addiction is a growing problem and doctors need training in dealing with it, claims the Centre for Online Addiction.
5a) [ ] The line between work and private life is much more blurred, now that email provides a 24-hour link between employers and employees.
b) [ ] Over 30% of office workers admit to checking their email in the evenings or at weekends.

The rise of technology addiction

A

¹ _a)_ It seems that we just can't leave our mobile phones or computers alone. Both adults and children are displaying signs of addiction to their gadgets. And if the trend continues, some psychologists warn the consequences for 'normal' personal and work relationships could be significant.

B

² .... It estimates that 6–10% of the 190 million Internet users in the US have an unhealthy dependency on gadgets such as mobile phones and computers.

C

³ .... The survey lists: using text messages or email when face-to-face interaction would be more appropriate; limiting time with friends and family to tend to your email or to surf the Internet; an inability to leave home without a mobile phone, or to relax without constantly checking email; and paying more attention to gadgets than what is happening in real life.

D

⁴ .... "I meet people who really cannot put their mobile phones down for fear of missing an email or a text message – even when there will be a negative consequence to their doing so," he explains.

E

"The compulsion to monitor these devices is as powerful as an addiction to alcohol or drugs," Dr Carr continues. However, unlike alcohol and drugs, Dr Carr believes that this communication addiction can usually be overcome by relatively simple methods. "This means setting limits for the amount of time spent on email, developing boundaries, such as time when you do not answer email or phone calls," he advises. "What is important is to establish a manageable relationship with technology such that it does not dominate your life."

F

With children, and for their parents, the situation is perhaps more worrying. All that time spent glued to their mobile phones and computer screens is taking time away from a particularly important activity, namely spending time together as a family.

G

The statistical findings of the survey are telling. 16–20-year-olds spend an average of just under four hours a day using technology. This compares with two hours a day spent with their families. Over 60% of the parents interviewed want to spend at least twice as much time with their children as the average.

H

In the Akehurst household, Andrew (17) and Nate (14) spend over six hours on their computers every day, according to their mother, Julie. "Andrew is up until the early hours on his laptop. Nate goes straight to the computer when he comes home. Andrew ends up missing various family events because he sleeps late into the morning, or even afternoon. And I can't remember the last time Nate told me about how his school day was." Julie is not overly worried by her situation but feels she is losing touch with her sons.

I

"Teenagers have always sought time alone – listening to music, reading and so on. Instant messaging and emailing is just another of these activities," says Dr Eileen Palser, a child psychologist from a San Francisco Hospital. Her latest book is entitled _Was it really any different when we were young?_ Dr Palser clearly thinks the current situation with teenagers is not significantly any different than that in the past. "They need time to develop into individuals – and they'll only ever do this out of their parents' company."

J

One aspect that Dr Palser acknowledges is more worrying is one of parental control. In the survey, almost 70% of parents felt that the use of technology makes it harder for parents to know what is going on in their children's lives. A third of parents interviewed felt the need to keep up with technology was a burden on the family budget. "In the past, parents could easily monitor what, for example, their children watched on TV," concedes Dr Palser. "The Internet has removed that ability as now, practically anything is available. And not all of it meets with parents' approval."

K

Dr Palser also reminds us of the upsides to the gadgets that surround our children. "Mobile phones and email make it easier to stay in touch when away from home," she points out. "Many parents have become accustomed to being in constant touch with their children. Besides, mobile phones are not particularly expensive these days."

Choose the best topic sentence a)–c) for each paragraph 1–3.

1 .... From our favourite TV programmes to our tastes in politics, we rarely agree. In the past, this has provided us with material for arguments at the dinner table while our wives and family watch us with dismay.
   a) My brother and I have never been on the same wavelength.
   b) My parents have always disapproved of my lifestyle.
   c) My father and mother have never seemed to have much in common.

2 .... Look at any group of people and you will see a range of facial expressions, hand and body movements. Each is expressing an additional meaning to the words being spoken.
   a) Speaking on the telephone isn't a satisfying means of communication.
   b) Email can be a dangerous form of communication.
   c) A surprising amount of human communication is non-verbal.

3 .... I often ask myself what they are doing. On the underground there is no signal. Is it a game? Do they have a very untidy address book? What am I missing out on?
   a) Travelling on public transport nowadays, it is common to see passengers playing with mobile phones.
   b) Loud phone conversations on public transport are a typical annoyance of the 21st century.
   c) It seems that no one can travel anywhere nowadays without their mobiles.

 Choose the best two supporting sentences for topic sentences 1–3.

1 It is often said that women gossip more than men.
   a) There is no scientific proof to back this claim.
   b) Men are more likely to butt in during meetings.
   c) However, is it just a dated stereotype?

2 The last time I had a row with my friend, we didn't speak for a month afterwards.
   a) We eventually made up, but things have never been the same since.
   b) We had fallen out over him chatting up an ex-girlfriend of mine.
   c) I split up with my girlfriend soon after that.

3 My son and daughter seem to spend most of their time together bickering.
   a) Being twins, they share a lot of their toys.
   b) It drives me mad at times.
   c) They constantly argue about everything, from toys to TV programmes.

 a) Look at these topic sentences from an article on how to communicate effectively. Match them to each group of supporting sentence prompts.

> Communication is a two-way process.
> Be articulate in your speaking.
> Organise your ideas in your mind before attempting to communicate them.
> Communication is central to everything we do.
> Firstly, choose the right time and the right place.

1 **Topic sentence:** ....
   Supporting sentences:
   ● Every day / speak to people / home and work.
   ● have conversations / send emails / hold meetings.
   ● Learning / communicate effectively / essential.

2 **Topic sentence:** ....
   Supporting sentences:
   ● need to discuss something sensitive / somewhere you can't be overheard.
   ● Alternatively / speaking to a large group of people / somewhere large so everyone can hear.

3 **Topic sentence:** ....
   Supporting sentences:
   ● Choose three main ideas / focus on those.
   ● If / important speech / practise.

4 **Topic sentence:** ....
   Supporting sentences:
   ● Avoid mumbling.
   ● Avoid negative facial expressions.
   ● Make eye contact.

5 **Topic sentence:** ....
   Supporting sentences:
   ● Listen carefully / other people.
   ● If / not / understand / ask people to repeat ideas.

b) Write an article about effective communication.
● Use your answers to **10a)**.
● Write full paragraphs using the supporting sentence prompts in **10a)**.
● Add further supporting sentences if necessary.
● Add two paragraphs using your own ideas.
● Remember to use a topic sentence in each new paragraph.
● Read and check for mistakes.
● Give your article to your teacher next class.

> Tick the things you can do in English in the Reading and Writing Progress Portfolio, p88.

Competition entries

Reading a competition about inspirational people
Writing using monolingual dictionaries
Review cleft sentences: *what* and *it* clauses

 1 Read the competition entries and introduction. Paragraphs 1–4 start with a different technique in order to attract the reader's attention. Match paragraphs 1–4 to techniques a)–d).

a) Tell a vivid personal story. ....

b) Ask a provocative question. ....

c) Use an appropriate quotation. ....

d) Present a surprising fact. ....

1 A recent survey reported that the most influential person in your life when it comes to career decisions is ... your mum! The old adage of 'following in your father's footsteps' has gone, it seems. This got us thinking about who the most influential people were in our lives, so last week we asked: *Who has influenced your life the most? Who inspires you on a daily basis?* Here are the best answers.

2 Will you just write me off as another celebrity-obsessed idiot if I say my greatest inspiration has been the industrious chef, Jamie Oliver?

I hope not, because it's true. As a paediatric dietician, my day-to-day work involves advising children (and their parents) on how to eat healthily. It can be a thankless task – some people seem to care so little about their, or their children's health.

Some may think Jamie is just another rich chef, churning out recipe books and TV shows for personal profit. However, I think that's far from the truth. Since he first gained fame in 1998, Jamie seems to have made it a personal mission to get our country eating more healthily. The most important of these, from my point of view, is his ongoing campaign to wean children off the junk-food culture that pervades British schools. What he has done is quite incredible and it is an inspiration to see someone using their talent and fame for good. Thank you, Jamie.

Robert Preston, London

3 I was in the last year of school, destined, without a doubt, to fail my final exams and end up jobless. Then one day, we had a supply teacher for a lesson on Shakespeare. As we shuffled into the classroom reluctantly retrieving our copies of *Hamlet* from our backpacks, she briefly introduced herself and directed us to put all books away and push our desks to the edge of the room.

What followed was an electrifying 90 minutes involving a courtroom role-play at the trial of Hamlet, with each of us taking roles as defender, prosecutor and witnesses. I'm not sure what it taught me about English literature but it awoke a fascination with the law that has never faded. I went on to pass my exams, study law at university, and three years ago I qualified as a criminal barrister.

I sometimes wonder where I'd be had she not appeared in our classroom that day, and whether I could contact her to thank her. If, by some infinitesimal chance you're reading this Ms Secker, thank you.

Sally Mercer, Nottingham

4 'Be around the people you want to be like, because you will be like the people you are around.'

I read this quote somewhere but have no idea where. It sums up exactly what I feel about people who inspire and influence me – namely, all my friends. I have three very close friends, all of whom I see at least once a week. We're really involved in and empathise with what each other is doing. We are constantly swapping advice on careers, relationships and other aspects of life. It is my friends that I always turn to when life is at a low point and conversely, they've always been with me to celebrate its highs.

James MacAndrew, Edinburgh

 2 What do you think words 1–6 from the extract mean? Choose the best answer.

1 adage	a) proverb	b) job	c) duty
2 industrious	a) famous	b) hard-working	c) confident
3 churn out	a) sell enthusiastically	b) write carefully	c) produce quickly
4 infinitesimal	a) lucky	b) very small	c) amazing
5 namely	a) specifically	b) for example	c) the names of
6 aspects	a) feelings	b) stages	c) parts

Reading and Writing Portfolio 2

 3 A monolingual dictionary, such as *Cambridge Advanced Learner's Dictionary*, can be an important tool for your writing. Look at the headings and the extracts and then match sentences 1–7 to gaps a)–g).

1 Example sentences are shown in *italics* in the entry for a word/phrase.

2 If the word has a different spelling in British or American English, the variant spelling is shown.

3 A word/phrase may be followed by a 'guideword' (a word/phrase, often in capital letters). This means the word has two or more main meanings and there is at least one other entry for that word.

4 Smaller differences in meanings between words are shown by separate numbered definitions.

5 Look for fixed phrases and idioms listed on separate lines.

6 Cross-references help you learn more vocabulary connected to a word. They often refer to words with a related or contrasting meaning.

7 'Labels' sometimes give you important information about how words/phrases are used, for example how formal it is or whether it is more common in British or American English.

CHECK THE SPELLING OF WORDS

a) ....

paediatrician *UK, US* **pediatrician**
/piːdiəˈtrɪʃən/ *noun* a doctor who
has special training in medical care
for children

CHECK THE MEANING OF WORDS

b) ....

follow GO /gəʊ/, *US* /goʊ/ *verb*
to move behind someone or
something and go where they go:
I knew I was being followed.

c) ....

• **follow in *sb's* footsteps**
to do the same thing as someone
else did previously: *She followed in
her mother's footsteps, starting her
own business.*

d) ....

close RELATIONSHIP /kləʊs/ *adj*
1 having direct family connections
or shared beliefs: *They only invited
close relatives to the wedding.*
2 describes people who know each
other very well: *Adam is a close friend
of mine.*

CHECK HOW WORDS/PHRASES ARE USED

e) ....

f) ....

infinitesimal /ɪnfɪnəˈtesəməl/ *adj*
FORMAL extremely small: *Scientists
measured infinitesimal levels of
radiation in the atmosphere.*

EXPAND YOUR VOCABULARY

g) ....

empathy /ˈempəθiː/ *noun* the ability
to share someone else's feelings or
experiences by imagining what it
would be like to be in their situation.
→ Compare **sympathy**

 4 Use a dictionary to complete the table with these words. Then add the missing spellings.

~~honour~~	defense	jewelry	metre
moustache	tire		

British English	American English
honour	_honor_
....	....
....	....
....	....
....	....
....	....

5 Match these guidewords to their meanings in this dictionary entry.

> ~~ACCIDENT~~   HAPPEN   SEASON
> LOWER   BE DEFEATED

fall [1] _ACCIDENT_ /ˈæksɪdənt/ *verb* to suddenly go down onto the ground or towards the ground unintentionally: *He fell badly and broke his leg.*

fall [2] .... *verb* to become lower in size, amount of strength: *Demand for luxury cars has fallen dramatically.*

fall [3] .... *verb* to be beaten: *The government fell after the death of their charismatic leader.*

fall [4] .... *verb* to come at a particular time: *My birthday falls on Friday this year.*

fall [5] .... US (UK **autumn**) *noun* the period of time after summer and before winter: *The leaves are amazing in New England in the fall.*

 6 Use a dictionary to match the following fixed phrases and idioms using *fall* to meanings 1–6.

> ~~fall about (laughing)~~   fall short
> fall into someone's trap
> fall on hard times   fall from grace
> nearly fall off your chair

1 ..*fall about (laughing)*.. UK INFORMAL to laugh uncontrollably

2 .... when you do something which makes people in authority stop liking or admiring you

3 .... to get into a difficult situation by trusting someone

4 .... INFORMAL to be extremely surprised

5 .... to lose your money and start to have a difficult life

6 .... to fail to reach a desired amount or standard, causing disappointment

7 Are words/phrases 1–6 informal or formal? Match them to meanings a)–f).

1 partake ..*formal*..
2 chilled ....
3 filch ....
4 parsimonious ....
5 strop ....
6 expound ....

a) steal
b) relaxed
c) to become involved (with sth)
d) unwilling to spend money
e) to give detailed explanation
f) a bad mood

 8 Read this competition entry. Look at the underlined words/ phrases and use a monolingual dictionary to rewrite them more appropriately.

I [1]pondered this question for some time but eventually decided it was obvious. It may be a [2]clishé but the person who has inspired me most is my husband. His [3]encouragment and support have [4]effected me in so many ways. [5]When ever I have a problem, I can always [6]rely of him to [7]talk the sense. He is the most [8]level-minded [9]chap I know – calm in even the most difficult situations. Without him, I wouldn't be [10]half a woman I am.

9 **a)** Think of someone who has inspired you, or greatly influenced your life. Make notes in the table.

who the person is	
how they have inspired you	
what you do/have done as a result	

b) Think of a way to begin your writing to engage the reader. Use one of the ideas in **1** or your own.

c) Write your competition entry.

- Use your notes in **9a)**.
- Start your competition entry effectively.
- Use a monolingual dictionary to check your spelling, use of language and to find some original words/phrases.
- Read and check for mistakes.
- Give your entry to your teacher next class.

> Tick the things you can do in English in the Reading and Writing Progress Portfolio, p88.

A proposal

Reading a proposal for gym membership
Writing putting forward ideas in a proposal
Review introductory *it*; inversion

1 Joanne is head of her company's social committee. She asked staff what they wanted as part of group membership to a new gym. Read her notes. Which point is not essential? Why?

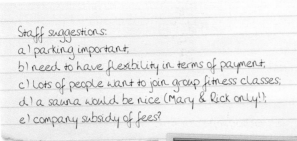

Staff suggestions:
a) parking important;
b) need to have flexibility in terms of payment;
c) lots of people want to join group fitness classes;
d) a sauna would be nice (Mary & Rick only!);
e) company subsidy of fees?

new   reply reply all forward   delete spam   check mail   print

Introduction
The social committee has investigated the possibility of taking advantage of reduced-rate group memberships at two local gyms, encouraging employees to get regular exercise. This proposal looks at the differences between two local gyms: To-the-Max and Work Out.

Facilities
Both gyms are large and well equipped. Work Out is the larger of the two gyms and includes a 25-metre pool together with a sauna and spa area. To-the-Max, on the other hand, separates its cardio gym from the weight-training area, which would be more pleasant for those wanting to do only cardio exercise. Although it does not have a sauna or spa, its locker and shower facilities have only just been renovated and are spacious and attractive. Finally, a key difference is that To-the-Max has its own car park with over 200 spaces. In contrast, Work Out does not provide a car park, but there is usually free parking in the streets surrounding the gym.

Group fitness
Only two staff members indicated they would like a sauna, while a large number of staff indicated that they are very interested in attending group fitness classes. Both gyms have a good range of these. However, not only does To-the-Max have a more varied programme, it also has more group fitness studios.

Cost and flexibility
To-the-Max is the most expensive, costing £20 per person per month, while Work Out costs £15. However, the two gyms differ in terms of membership schemes. To-the-Max has the benefit of offering a more flexible membership scheme because employees can opt out at any stage after the first month, whereas Work Out requires a minimum six-month membership before it is possible to opt out. A further point in relation to cost is that staff would appreciate a financial contribution from the company for those who take up a fitness programme.

Conclusion and recommendation
Although To-the-Max is not quite as large and as well equipped as Work Out, it is thought to be the most suitable gym for our employees. To-the-Max is more expensive, but a company subsidy will help offset the cost. Furthermore, the possibility of being able to cancel membership after one month offers greater flexibility. I recommend that we take out a group membership with To-the-Max.

2 Read Joanne's email outlining her proposal quickly and answer these questions.

1 Which gym does she recommend?
2 Does it have everything staff asked for?

 3 Read again and answer these questions.

1 What are the main differences in fitness facilities between the two gyms?

....

....

2 In what way are the To-the-Max fitness programmes better?

....

....

3 Which gym allows people to give up their membership sooner if they want to?

....

....

4 What would help make gym fees cheaper?

....

....

5 What key advantages does To-the-Max offer?

....

....

4 Read the proposal again and use the context to match these words/phrases to definitions a)–f).

| in terms of   subsidy   renovate   opt out |
| take up (sth)   offset |

a) repair and redecorate a building that is in bad

   condition ....

b) start doing a hobby or an activity in your free

   time ....

c) create a more balanced situation ....

d) money given by an organisation to pay part of

   the cost of something ....

e) with regard to, concerning ....

f) choose not to be part of an activity ....

Help with Writing Putting forward ideas in a proposal

 5 **a)** Look at these sentences. Choose the phrases used in the proposal.

● To-the-Max, ¹*although/on the other hand*, separates its cardio gym from its weight-training area.
● This proposal looks at the ²*differences about/ differences between* two local gyms.
● ³*Although/However* it does not have a sauna or spa, its locker and shower facilities have only just been renovated.
● A ⁴*key difference/total difference* is that To-the-Max has its own car park.
● ⁵*Although/In contrast*, Work Out does not provide a car park, ⁶*but/however* there is usually free parking in the streets.
● Work Out is ⁷*larger/the larger* of the two gyms.
● ⁸*However/But*, not only does To-the-Max have a ⁹*more/most* varied programme, it also has more group fitness studios.
● The two gyms ¹⁰*differ in/differ about* terms of membership schemes.
● Only two staff members indicated they would like a sauna, ¹¹*while/on the other hand* a large number signalled an interest in a range of fitness classes.

b) Choose the correct answer.

The correct language in **5a)** is used to:

1 show reasons and results.
2 contrast and compare information.
3 indicate that extra information has been added.

c) Match the correct words/phrases in **5a)** to descriptions a)–g).

a) a verb used to compare two things ..*10*..

b) nouns used to compare two things .... , ...

c) a noun phrase that includes a zero or indefinite

   article and a comparative adjective ....

d) a noun phrase that includes a definite article and

   a comparative adjective ....

e) adverbial linkers of contrast .... , ... , ...

f) conjunctions showing concession .... , ...

g) a conjunction of contrast ....

6 Fill in each gap with a correct word/phrase from **5a)**. There is sometimes more than one possible answer.

1 The _key difference_ between the two fitness programmes is that I use the rowing machine more.

2 You should aim to increase your heart rate. _____ , if you start to feel faint or dizzy, please stop immediately.

3 Frank did a cardio workout, _____ Scott did weight training.

4 The two personal trainers _____ terms of their approach to fitness.

5 _____ they had an easy workout, they still felt tired afterwards.

6 I think my gym offers _____ interesting range of classes than others.

7 I go to the gym about twice a week. Suzanne, _____ , goes every weekday.

8 I don't really like the fitness classes, _____ I enjoy cardio training on my own.

9 The 6 p.m. class is definitely _____ crowded of the two evening fitness classes.

10 _____ I often don't feel like going, once I get to the gym I usually enjoy the workout.

 7 **a)** You have been asked to write a proposal for the location of a company's new coffee area. There are two options: an unused storeroom or an unused office. Read the notes for the proposal. Decide which location you think would be best.

b) Write a proposal using the notes or your own ideas.

- Decide how to divide the information into key sections, and think of a heading for each section.
- Include an introduction and conclusion.
- Make a suggestion about the espresso machine and water cooler.
- Make a specific recommendation about which location to turn into a coffee area.
- Use the words/phrases in **5a)**.
- Read and check for mistakes.
- Give your proposal to your teacher next class.

storeroom
✓ conveniently situated for all staff
✓ already has running water
✓ cheap to renovate
✗ small – hardly any room for seating
✗ no windows

office
✓ spacious – lots of natural light
✓ room for seating – but need to buy tables and chairs
✗ not conveniently situated – it's near the manager's office
✗ no running water
✗ expensive to renovate

Staff and management comments:
- most staff happy with either location – just want separate coffee area
- if near manager's office, will he overhear conversations?
- three or four staff think natural light is important
- several staff want an espresso machine and water cooler
- manager wants to keep costs down

Tick the things you can do in English in the Reading and Writing Progress Portfolio, p88.

A website post

Reading a website post
Writing ways to organise discussion writing
Review near synonyms

 Read the comment on the website of *Cultural Wave* magazine.
Are these statements true (T) or false (F)?

1 ☐ The writer wants the magazine to stay as it is.

2 ☐ She doesn't like a recent change to the magazine.

3 ☐ She is a regular reader of *Cultural Wave*.

4 ☐ She probably watches reality TV quite rarely.

Forum >> Cultural Wave >> Discussion

| Login | Message | << Older Topic | Newer Topic >> |

📄 Disappointed - Today 2:03 pm

Diana
Senior member

Posts: 12

Joined: 29 Aug

Last on: Today 12:00pm

Status: **ONLINE**

a) **"Unhappy is the country that needs heroes."** This is a quote from the play *Galileo* by German playwright Bertolt Brecht, which has been very much in my thoughts in the past couple of months, as Cultural Wave has begun to include more articles on celebrities and their lifestyles. I can only imagine that you have decided to increase the gossip quotient in order to make more sales. Is this trend going to continue?

While I think this is a disappointing shift in focus for a magazine that has included some intriguing reports on trends in our society, b) **I believe it raises the broader issue of why we are all so obsessed with celebrities and their every move.** Everywhere we look in the media, we find yet another story about some singer, movie star, or sports personality who has done something eccentric – or, even worse, has done nothing at all except go to the supermarket without make-up.

c) **Why are we so captivated by these people?** I believe that as long as we all invest time in, and pay particular attention to celebrity lives, we will stop living our own lives. We talk about celebrities as though they were our best friends and I sometimes wonder whether that stops us from forming good friendships with the people around us.

d) **Furthermore, in believing we have some kind of relationship with the famous person**, we possibly begin to form a very superficial view of what a relationship of any kind involves. It is very easy to follow the ups and downs, and tantrums and triumphs of your favourite rock star from a safe distance. I am not so sure their fans would cope so well with the dirty reality of close proximity to their adored one.

e) **Another point I find irritating is** that many of these 'celebrities' are nothing more than no-talents who have no particular abilities. Many are rejects from the latest reality TV programme who have done nothing more in life than be filmed in a house while they swear at their housemates. Even those celebrities who do have talent should not be called upon to make observations on the state of the world. The ability to kick a football doesn't provide the kind of insight that will solve the problem of global warming.

f) **Conversely, I am fully aware that many will disagree with me.** They will argue that celebrities fulfil a useful role in society because they give us someone to look up to. However, in all seriousness, how many of these people can you really respect? Alternatively, some people will say that reading about celebrities is nothing more than harmless fun. I don't agree. I think there is a price to pay in terms of how we deal with our own lives.

g) **So please, can we have** a little less of the trivial celebrity chat (I'm realistic enough to know that you have to keep some in), and a return to more thought-provoking discussion of culture?

Disappointed Diana from Devon

✉ Post a reply

Read the comment again. What does the writer say about the following topics? Tick (✓) the correct answer.

1 Information that is reported about celebrities:
   a) is often trivial and not really news.
   b) aims to publicise films, CDs or TV programmes connected with the celebrity.
   c) doesn't go into enough detail.

2 We can:
   a) try to live the same glamorous lives as celebrities and get into debt.
   b) spend so much time and energy following celebrities' lives that we ignore friends and family.
   c) spend too much time talking to our friends about celebrities.

3 On the nature of the relationship we have with celebrities:
   a) we begin to believe it is meaningful, but it isn't.
   b) we find it difficult when we are really close to them.
   c) the more we find out about them, the angrier they make us feel.

4 On the level of ability of some celebrities:
   a) while their public relations skills are good, they have limited sporting skills.
   b) many are rejected from TV programmes.
   c) some are talented, but a lot of them have no skill beyond the fact that they have appeared on TV.

5 Celebrities:
   a) have their place, and reading about them can be entertaining.
   b) are important in society and their actions don't hurt anyone.
   c) provide us with someone to respect.

6 On the magazine's content:
   a) deeper insights into celebrity lifestyles should be added.
   b) all discussion of celebrities should be avoided.
   c) the amount of celebrity gossip should be reduced.

 Match these near synonyms from the website post.

> chat   trivial   ability   personality   insight
> thought-provoking   captivated by   look up to

1 gossip _chat_
2 respect ....
3 obsessed with ....
4 celebrity ....
5 observations ....
6 superficial ....
7 talent ....
8 intriguing ....

Help with Writing Ways to organise discussion writing

4 **a) The writer uses different techniques to introduce and structure her main ideas. Match techniques 1–7 to the phrases in bold in the website post.**

1 The writer adds an extra idea to support her argument. _e)_
2 She uses a rhetorical question. ....
3 She refers to opposing points of view. ....
4 She makes a general statement of her opinion to outline the issue under discussion. ....
5 She sums up with a call for action. ....
6 She builds on a point previously made in order to express the next point. ....
7 She uses a quote to create interest and introduce the topic. ....

b) Look again at the website post. Which of these structures is most suitable for discussion writing?

1 interesting information → different points in support of the writer's point of view → opposing points of view → conclusion and call for action → general statement on the topic
2 opposing points of view → different points in support of the writer's point of view → general statement on the topic → interesting information → conclusion and call for action
3 interesting information → general statement on the topic → different points in support of the writer's opinion → opposing points of view → conclusion and call for action

5 Read extracts 1–7, which are taken from a reply to Diana. Match them to techniques a)–e).

① Hi Diana. What annoys *me* is the cultural arrogance of people who say they don't read these magazines.

② This points to the current debate about the role of gossip magazines.

③ On the other hand, I know many people see this issue in a very different way.

④ I think some people take the whole issue of celebrity magazines more seriously than is necessary.

⑤ While some gossip magazines worry about the influence of the Internet, sales figures are still very healthy compared to other weekly publications.

⑥ All I ask is that I be left in peace to enjoy my weekly catch-up with the rich and famous.

⑦ What's more, reading about celebrities can be a good thing for people who are lonely.

✉ Post a reply

a) quote/interesting information ___5___

b) general statement about the topic _____

c) points in support of the writer's

point of view _____ , _____ , _____

d) opposing point of view _____

e) conclusion/call to action _____

6 **a)** Choose one of these topics or your own idea. Make notes in the table.

- 'Being famous' has more disadvantages than advantages.
- Anyone can become a celebrity these days.
- Celebrities provide us with good role models.

point 1	● main idea
	● details/examples
point 2	● main idea
	● details/examples
point 3	● main idea
	● details/examples
point 4	● main idea
	● details/examples

b) Decide how you will begin writing about the topic or issue. Find, or think of one of these:

- a quote.
- a rhetorical question (formal or informal).
- an interesting fact or statistic.
- an interesting result from a survey or questionnaire.
- a controversial statement.

c) Write a website post about the topic or issue.

- Use your notes from **6a)**.
- Structure your main ideas in an organised way.
- Include some opposing points of view.
- Read and check for mistakes.
- Give your website post to your teacher next class.

Tick the things you can do in English in the Reading and Writing Progress Portfolio, p88.

An article

Reading an article
Writing personalising language
Review reflexive pronouns

 1 Read the article about volunteer work in a developing country. Choose the best answers.

1 The writer's main aim is to ...
  a) describe the sights and sensations of his month away.
  b) recruit more volunteers for Kenya.
  c) highlight the value of volunteer work.

2 By the end of the month, the writer felt ...
  a) appreciative of the experience he had had.
  b) that he didn't want to go home.
  c) very sad about the children he worked with.

 2 Read the article again. Are these sentences true (T) or false (F)?

1 ☐ Damian thinks many people are unsure how effective donations to charity really are.

2 ☐ He believes he was 'privileged' because he was much richer than most people in Kenya.

3 ☐ All the children in the orphanage suffered from AIDS.

4 ☐ Damian is full of admiration for Emma.

5 ☐ He managed to improve the children's English in order to communicate more easily with them.

6 ☐ Everyone from the neighbourhood sang Beatles songs at the concert.

7 ☐ Damian felt the concert was a success because the singing was very good.

8 ☐ He feels that anyone has the potential to help people in developing countries.

3 What do these words/phrases mean as they are used in the article? Choose the best answer.

1 desperate
  a) increasing   b) huge   c) very serious
2 privileged
  a) honoured   b) frightened   c) well-paid
3 pitched in
  a) began to cry   b) began to help   c) watched
4 drawback
  a) disadvantage   b) reward   c) regret
5 immeasurably
  a) the same   b) slightly more   c) extremely
6 endure
  a) stop   b) suffer   c) help

Help with Writing Personalising language

 4 Read the article again. Each paragraph has a different purpose. Match paragraphs A–E to sentences 1–5.

1 Give background information on the general situation. ....

2 Give the reader something to think about. ....

3 Describe the writer's reaction to the situation. ....

4 Provide background and get the reader's attention. ....

5 Tell an anecdote. ....

 5 The writer uses different pronouns to personalise his writing. Answer these questions.

1 The two main pronouns in paragraph A are *we* and *I*. Who does *we* refer to?

....

....

2 Why does the writer begin with *we* rather than beginning by talking about himself?

....

....

3 In paragraphs C and D, *we* and *I* are used again. Who does *we* refer to in these paragraphs?

....

....

4 What is the first pronoun used in paragraph C? Why does he use this?

....

....

5 In paragraph E, what pronoun does the writer use to address the reader? Why does he do this?

....

....

HHA Helping Hands Abroad – *Making a real difference*

The neighbourhood Beatles concert

By Damian Rogers

A

We all worry about poor people in developing countries because their need is desperate. Sometimes we give money to charity, but wonder if it really makes a difference. The problems always seem so overwhelming. Earlier this year, I was privileged to experience third-world poverty first-hand. Yes, I used the word 'privileged'. Without doubt, this was one of the richest and most rewarding months of my entire life – I found out how much difference even the smallest gesture can make.

B

I spent a month doing volunteer work in Kenya at an orphanage for children who had lost their parents and relatives to AIDS. Some of the children are themselves infected with HIV, but they are too young to really understand that. While the overall situation of the orphanage is heartbreaking, these kids are full of life! I just pitched in and did what I could. Sometimes I helped in the classroom, sometimes I took sick kids to the local hospital for check-ups. A couple of kids got quite ill and I helped to look after them. One girl, little Emma, was very sick and in quite a bit of pain for a few days. She is only eight years old, but her bravery was awe-inspiring. She never once complained and always managed to give me a weak smile.

C

For myself, the only drawback was my inability to speak Swahili. I'm hopeless at languages, so I never really made the effort. The kids at the orphanage spoke some English, but I would love to have been able to really communicate with them in their language. Still, these children also spoke the language of friendship and generosity with total fluency, so in the end, we communicated extremely well. There is no doubt that their ability to give has made me immeasurably richer than I was before we went to Kenya.

D

My biggest success was in the field of music. I took my guitar with me and taught the kids three Beatles songs (the Beatles are still big in Kenya!): *Yellow Submarine*, *Help* and *Yesterday*. In my last week at the orphanage, we held a Beatles concert and a huge number of people from the local neighbourhood came bringing food and drink. Our concert turned into a neighbourhood party and the kids had a great time. I think I had the best time of all knowing that in my brief time there, I'd managed to bring a bit of joy into their lives.

E

So, you can see that just one man with a guitar can make a difference to people who have to endure incredible hardship. The difference isn't always a question of money. It's just a question of giving something – your time, your talent, your attention – giving of yourself. It does make a difference to these people, but more importantly, what you get back from them will make a huge and positive difference to you.

6 Complete this introduction and conclusion to an article with an appropriate pronoun or possessive adjective.

> ¹ _We_ all hate it when charities phone ² .... to ask for a donation. They always call at dinner time and expect ³ .... to listen to a long-winded explanation. ⁴ .... used to find this sort of thing irritating until ⁵ .... spent some time working for a local charity. Being on the receiving end of other people's irritation changed ⁶ .... point of view.

> In summary, ⁷ _my_ message is very straightforward. What ⁸ .... appreciated was people who were prepared to be civil to ⁹ .... ¹⁰ .... didn't mind if they couldn't make a donation, so long as they were prepared to be polite to ¹¹ .... So, the next time someone calls ¹² .... to ask for a donation, ¹³ .... should really treat the person as ¹⁴ .... ¹⁵ .... would hope to be treated.

7 Rewrite the <u>underlined</u> phrases in these introductory and concluding paragraphs. Make them more interesting by involving the reader and personalising the language.

> *We are all concerned*
> ¹<s>There is general concern</s> about the fact that young people have no sense of the value of things. ²<u>It is sometimes felt</u> that everything is handed to them on a plate. ³<u>When younger, the current writer</u> wanted everything to be easy. ⁴<u>There were feelings of antipathy towards his</u> parents when they insisted on doing volunteer work with a charity during the school or university holidays. ⁵<u>The writer questioned the need to waste time doing unpaid work</u>.

> *I can't say*
> ⁶<s>It cannot be said</s> that the experience did ⁷<u>the writer</u> any harm at all. ⁸<u>Some extraordinary people were met</u>, some of whom ⁹<u>the writer knows</u> will be friends for life. This goes to show that ¹⁰<u>it is a good idea</u> to always remain open to experiences, particularly ones where ¹¹<u>there is the possibility of involvement</u> with new and interesting people.

8 **a)** You have been asked to write an article for your school's website. The topic of the article is 'Learning something new is an adventure'. Make notes in the table.

what you learned	
what the situation was	
how you felt	
an anecdote associated with the experience	

b) Write your article.

- Use your notes from **8a)**.
- Involve the reader in your introduction. Can you refer to a common experience? Is there a question you can ask?
- Personalise the article using ideas from **5**.
- Structure your information in clear paragraphs, with a clear focus for each.
- Finish by asking the reader to think about something.
- Read and check for mistakes.
- Give your article to your teacher next class.

> Tick the things you can do in English in the Reading and Writing Progress Portfolio, p88.

Letters of complaint

Reading three letters of complaint
Writing a letter of complaint
Review phrasal verbs; relative clauses

1 Read the letters quickly. Answer the questions.

Which letter(s):

1 is to the Advertising Complaints Authority? ....

2 is to an Internet service provider? ....

3 is to a property letting agency? ....

4 are about something paid for regularly? .... , ...

5 is about something not paid for? ....

A

Dear Sir/Madam,
I wish to complain about the broadband speeds I am receiving from SpeedyNet. I have subscribed to your service (20MB/s) since March and pay £25 per month.

For the last eight weeks I have been suffering from slow speeds in the evening. The connection speed is almost always less than 2MB/s. This effectively makes my Internet connection useless in the evening, a peak time for me and my family.

I have called your company's helpline and no-one to whom I have spoken has been able to improve or rectify the situation. Instead, I have been told to just switch off my computer and modem, wait five minutes and then switch it on again. None of this has had any effect on the problem. [1]One woman I spoke to even implied I was lying! I would estimate I spent at least four hours on the phone to your customer and technical support departments.

[a)]**I would appreciate it if you could** contact me to advise me when/how you will resolve this problem. [2]Otherwise, I will be passing this matter to my solicitor for further action.

Yours faithfully,

M Green
Marty Green
[b)]**cc:** Office of Communications (OFCOM)

B

Dear Sir,
[3]I recently came across an ad for the Vanguard 4x4 car in the *Guardian* (15th June). I attach a photocopy of the advertisement [c)]**in question**.
In particular, [d)]**I would like to take issue with** the text of the advertisement that the Vanguard 4x4 is "a truly environmentally friendly vehicle". Furthermore, the advertisement states the car "has low emission rates".

The implication from these statements is that the Vanguard 4x4 results in little or no damage to the environment. [4]In addition, the Vanguard 4x4 is a SUV (Sports Utility Vehicle, or 4x4) and therefore in comparison to a compact car, will frequently consumes significantly more fuel. The advert fails to make this clear and implies that the Vanguard 4x4 is more environmentally friendly in relation to all vehicles.

This advertisement is another example of 'greenwashing' – misleading consumers regarding the environmental credentials of the companies.
I would appreciate your investigation of this advertisement and look forward to reading your reaction.

Yours faithfully,
Fen Starky
Fen Starky

C

Dear Miranda Letts,
On 21st February, we signed a nine-month contract to rent the above address. [e)]**Please find enclosed** a copy of the contract and terms.

At this time there were some problems in the house that we were assured would be resolved prior to our moving in. In particular, there was a leak in the roof, some carpet that needed [5]profesional cleaning and a faulty freezer that needed repair/replacement.

It is now two months since we moved into the property and none of these problems have been resolved. Phone calls to your office have been met with promises to visit the property and undertake necessary work. However, nothing has been done. [6]This is a totally unacceptable situation – you are horrible people who seem to have no ethics whatsoever!

If you do not [f)]**put matters right** within two weeks (or such another period as we may agree), I shall obtain quotations from reputable contractors to make necessary repairs. I shall deduct the cost of these repairs from future rent payments. [7]I'm sorry to have to resort to this measure, but I feel I have no choice.

I shall also be reporting this matter to Camden Council.

Yours sincerely,
Olivia Paxton   *Jack Mepstead*
Olivia Paxton
Jack Mepstead

Read the letters again and complete the table.

	letter A	letter B	letter C
background	*has been paying for broadband since March 2009 – £25/month*		
problem		*advertisement is misleading*	
effect			
solution			
warning			*will deduct cost from rent*

Help with Writing A letter of complaint

 Look at <u>underlined</u> phrases 1–7 in the letters. They are all features that are <u>not</u> useful in letters of complaint in English. Match them to advice a)–f).

a) avoid apologising – you are not in the wrong, so it is not necessary: ....

b) avoid grammar or spelling mistakes: .... , ...

c) do not threaten legal action unless it is particularly appropriate: ....

d) avoid rudeness: ....

e) if you are complaining about someone in particular, be as specific as possible: ....

f) avoid informal language (phrasal verbs, etc.): ....

 Sometimes phrasal verbs are acceptable in formal letters if they are very common or part of a useful phrase. Find one phrasal verb used appropriately in each letter.

letter A ....

letter B ....

letter C ....

5 **Match phrases a)–f) in bold in the letters to meanings 1–6.**

1 (the person/thing) being discussed ....

2 I am putting in this letter ....

3 I want you to ....

4 I disagree strongly with ....

5 resolve the problems ....

6 a copy of this letter has also been sent to ....

 Most phrasal verbs have a more formal equivalent. Replace the phrasal verbs in these sentences from letters of complaint with the correct form of these verbs.

~~upset~~	continue	resolve	invent
arrive	respect	review	wait

upsetting me

1 The situation is greatly ~~bringing me down~~.

2 I resent the implication that I am making up problems with this television.

3 Can you please go over your records and confirm whether this bill is correct?

4 I really cannot hang on any longer for you to solve this.

5 I have always looked up to your company for its ethical policies, but ...

6 I would appreciate your help in sorting out this problem as soon as possible.

7 The customer representative turned up an hour late for our meeting.

8 I must ask you not to keep on sending me threatening letters about payment.

7 Read this letter of complaint. The words/phrases in **bold** are inappropriate in some way. Rewrite the letter in your notebooks.

Dear Sir/Madam,

On 4th August ¹**me and three mates** went to Antonio's in Bond Street, London, for dinner. I had booked a table at 7.30 p.m. on the Internet. I ²**am putting in** a copy of this booking. We arrived at the restaurant at 7.25 p.m. We were told that a table would be ready within 15 ³**mins** and we were invited to wait in the bar until called.

At 8.15p.m. I noticed some people who had ⁴**turned up** after us being called to their table. I enquired as to whether our table was ready and was told that it was not. I asked why some people who had arrived after us had already been seated. ⁵**The rather rude woman told me** that they had booked a table at 8.00 p.m. but had threatened to leave if they were not seated. Since we had not complained, your restaurant seemed to have decided we could wait longer.

As you can imagine, I was rather ⁶**put out** by this situation. I immediately ⁷**canceled** my booking, we ⁸**stormed out of** the restaurant and, unable to find a suitable table elsewhere, we returned home. ⁹**You ruined our evening – thanks a lot!**

¹⁰**I apologise for writing this letter of complaint, but** I was extremely ¹¹**disapointed** by the service at Antonio's on this occasion. ¹²**I want you to explain what was going on.**

¹³**And you should expect to hear from my solicitor!**

¹⁴**Yours sincerely,**

Adam Cornish.

 8 a) You have just returned from a disastrous two-week package holiday. Think of reasons why your holiday was spoiled. Use the cartoons and your own ideas.

b) Make notes about your holiday in the table.

Background when you booked, what the advertisement said, how much you paid, etc.	
Problem the problems that were the fault of the holiday company	
Effect what the effect of the problems was	
Solution what you propose the holiday company should do about the problems	
Warning what action you will take if the holiday company does not resolve the situation	

c) Write your letter of complaint.

- Use your notes in **8b)**.
- Use the advice in **3**.
- Use formal language.
- Read and check for mistakes.
- Give your letter to your teacher next class.

Tick the things you can do in English in the Reading and Writing Progress Portfolio, p88.

Reading and Writing Portfolio 7

A review

Reading a book review
Writing cohesive devices
Review character adjectives

 1 Read the review of *The Girl of His Dreams*. What is the reviewer's impression of the book? Choose the best answer.

a) very favourable
b) mostly favourable with the occasional doubt
c) mildly positive, but quite negative in places

 2 **a)** Read again. Choose the best answers.

1 ....
a) The main character is a Venetian (policeman)/*private eye*.
b) He is *aggressive/hardworking*.

2 ....
a) A young girl *drowns/is shot*.
b) The girl's identity is *unknown/known*.
c) The story concerns *poor people in Venice/all levels of Venetian society*.

3 ....
a) The story is *gripping/unusual*.
b) Brunetti is *an eccentric/a convincing* character.
c) The writing is *complex/well-written*.

4 ....
a) The reviewer thinks this is
   a great crime story/a story of a great crime.
b) *The Girl of His Dreams needs/doesn't need* to
   be read as part of the series.
c) The reviewer *recommends/doesn't recommend*
   reading the rest of the series.

b) The writer organises his review into four sections. Match these headings to sections 1–4 in **2a)**.

> Story   Recommendation   Evaluation
> Introduction and background

 3 **a)** Read the review again and use the context to match these words to definitions a)–h).

> sumptuous   must-read   dedicated
> exasperating   satisfying   lucid   subtle
> multifaceted

a) extremely annoying ....
b) luxurious and showing wealth ....
c) not obvious ....
d) giving pleasure ....

e) consisting of many parts ....
f) clearly expressed and easy to understand ....
g) believing that something is important and giving a lot of
   time and energy to it ....
h) something so good, you have to read it ....

b) Which words in **3a)** does the reviewer use to describe:

1 the city? ....
2 the novel/the writing? .... , ... , ... , ...
3 the characters? .... , ... , ...

c) Match a word in **3a)** to these near synonyms from the book review.

1 fulfilling ....
2 multilayered ....
3 gorgeous ....
4 vivid ....

Help with Writing Cohesive devices

 4 **a)** Look at words/phrases 1–15 in **bold** in the review. What do they refer to? Fill in the table.

The Girl of His Dreams	Donna Leon	Brunetti	the writing
...1... , ...	...5... , ...	...10... , ...	...7... , ...
.... , ...		....	
.... , ...			
.... , ...			

b) Read these sentences about the language in **4a)**. Which one is not correct?

1 We use a variety of nouns, pronouns and possessive adjectives to link ideas between sentences.
2 We use a variety of nouns to make written language more interesting.
3 We use pronouns and possessive adjectives to avoid unnecessary repetition of nouns.
4 We use a variety of pronouns and possessive adjectives to make the order of the sentences clear.
5 We use a variety of nouns, pronouns and possessive adjectives to make written language more cohesive.

THE GIRL OF HIS DREAMS by Donna Leon

Not only a simple 'whodunit' …

Reviewed by Steven Shuttleworth

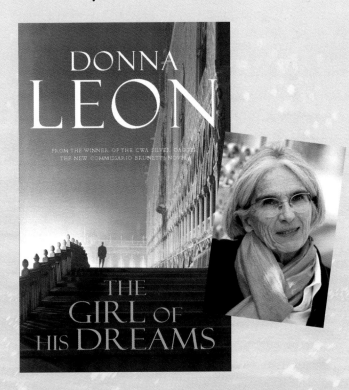

Venice is one of the most sumptuous cities in the world. Have you ever wanted to go there without having to leave home? The easiest way to have a quick trip to Venice is by reading one of Donna Leon's *Guido Brunetti* crime novels. This is a must-read series for lovers of crime fiction.

The Girl of His Dreams is the latest book in this series based around the Venetian police commissario, Guido Brunetti. Brunetti is an entirely original creation: a gifted and dedicated detective, who is also a loving family man that delights in his wife's mouth-watering cooking. He is surrounded by a now familiar cast of family members and colleagues who can be in turns both lovable and exasperating. Guido Brunetti is a very human detective you would like to get to know.

The Girl of His Dreams begins with a different kind of death – the funeral of Brunetti's mother. However, before long, there is a second death. This time a young girl is pulled from the waters of Venice's Grand Canal. She carries no identity and there is no record of a missing child. More mysterious is the gold jewellery that the girl is carrying. Brunetti and his colleague Ispettore Vianello set out to discover the identity of the victim as well as the cause of her death. This search takes them from the houses of well-to-do Venetians to the poverty of a gypsy camp outside the city. It is also a journey through the problems and prejudices of contemporary society.

[1]**This chapter in the continuing Brunetti saga** is without doubt one of the most enjoyable. [2]**It** is [3]**an enjoyable piece of crime fiction**, with a very definite mystery to unravel. The ending is very satisfying. However, *The Girl of His Dreams* is not only a simple [4]**whodunit**, but also contains all the usual joys we have come to expect from Donna Leon. The writing is lucid and there is the feeling of [5]**the writer** being in complete control of [6]**her** [7]**craft**. [8]**The descriptions** of Venice are extremely vivid, demonstrating Donna Leon's extraordinary ability to bring the gorgeous city to life. The characters in [9]**the book** are multifaceted, and, as such, very human. Brunetti is not [10]**a policeman** who deals in a world of black and white. [11]**His** is a world of subtle shades of grey and [12]**he** is all the more interesting for it. Finally, [13]**this** is [14]**a novel** that balances forces of darkness and light. [15]**It** reminds us that we live in a morally challenging world.

If you like a fulfilling crime story, then this book is for you. If you like a satisfying novel with multilayered characters of real depth and insight, then this book is also for you. I recommend getting hold of a copy as soon as you can. You don't have to have read the previous Brunetti novels to enjoy and appreciate *The Girl of His Dreams*. But then you might just want to go back to *Death at La Fenice* (the first) to savour the delights of this fantastic series from the beginning. Once you've read one Brunetti instalment, you'll want to rush out and get the rest.

Reading and Writing Portfolio 7

 5 Read an excerpt from a review of *Suffer the Little Children*. Replace the words/phrases in **bold** with words in the box. Sometimes there is more than one possible answer.

> ~~instalment~~   novel   she   mystery   it (x 2)   his (x 2)
> policeman   he   her (x 2)

> *instalment*
> *Suffer the Little Children* is the next fantastic ¹**book** in the Brunetti series. ²**Suffer the Little Children** centres around a crime that involves children and fertility. ³**Suffer the Little Children** is an intriguing ⁴**book** that keeps you guessing. Donna Leon shows ⁵**Donna Leon** is very much at home in Venice and ⁶**Donna Leon's** great love for the city is evident. ⁷**Donna Leon's** descriptions are nothing short of magical. Guido Brunetti shows all ⁸**Guido Brunetti's** determination to solve the crime. But ⁹**Guido Brunetti** is a ¹⁰**person** who knows when to stop for lunch and enjoy ¹¹**Guido Brunetti's** food. This ¹²**book** is another rare treat from Donna Leon.

 6 Complete this excerpt from another review. Sometimes there is more than one possible answer.

> ~~novel~~   Leon   his   tale   story   she (x 2)
> he   her   policeman   the writer's   it

> *Suffer the Little Children* is another gripping ¹ *novel* from Donna Leon. ² .... is an intriguing ³ .... that revolves around infertility and criminal goings-on. ⁴ .... builds the suspense with ⁵ .... usual skill. And the way ⁶ .... describes food will leave your mouth watering. Once again, it is a pleasure to be back in the company of Commissario Brunetti. It is rare to find such an amiable and charming ⁷ .... I feel like ⁸ .... and ⁹ .... family are good friends. This ¹⁰ .... maintains ¹¹ .... already high standard. How does ¹² .... do it?

 7 **a)** Think of a book or film you have enjoyed. Make notes in the table.

Introduction/ background • setting • author, director, actors, etc	
Story • main events • characters	
Evaluation • what you liked best • what you thought of the story, characters, etc.	
Recommendation	

b) Write your review.
- Use your notes from **7a)**.
- Make sure your opinion is clear in the recommendation, and check the grammar you use.
- Vary the kinds of words you use to talk about the book or film – use a monolingual dictionary to help.
- Read and check for mistakes.
- Give your review to your teacher next class.

> Tick the things you can do in English in the Reading and Writing Progress Portfolio, p88.

An informal email

Reading an informal email
Writing informal language
Review past verb forms with present meaning

From: Jamie@mail.net **To:** everyone

Subject: Queenstown bungy!

¹**Hi guys!**

a)<u>Sorry about the group email</u>, but you know how it is when you're travelling – no time for individual messages. ²**Sorry, sorry, sorry that** I've been so slack about sending messages. This holiday is full-on and it's hard finding the time to get into an Internet café.

³**Well**, you can see from the subject line where I've finally got to on my big New Zealand tour. Yes, that's right, I'm in Queenstown and I've done one of the things I set out to do on this holiday: the original bungy jump from Kawarau Bridge. b)<u>IT WAS AWESOME!</u> But really scary!

The bungy site is about 20 minutes out of town. I went out there feeling all cool and relaxed. "No worries," I thought. I paid my ticket and filled out the waiver forms and stuff, and the guy behind the counter kept saying "No refunds even if you don't jump."

"Yeah, yeah, yeah," I thought – there's no way that I'm going to back out of this! It's all ⁴**cool**.

After that, you get weighed and ⁵**stuff** like that and then I went up on to the walkway to get ready. A guy there ties you on to the rope and checks everything's OK. Up until that point, everything is sweet. But then … then I suddenly looked down at the river. Like, this was 43 metres down and suddenly I was terrified. c)<u>And I said</u> to myself "If only I hadn't bought the ticket!"

The operator could see I was beginning to freak out and he starts saying "It's OK, mate, it's OK." And I was thinking, "It's not OK, it's not OK! No way is it OK!" But I don't say anything. I just start to shake and I can't move. And the operator tells me to step out on to the platform and I say, "I'd rather not jump just now." But he says, "Come on, mate, take a deep breath – concentrate on the scenery." Somehow, d)<u>I manage to shuffle on to the platform</u>. And by now I'm saying, "I can't do it". And the operator says, "Yes, you can – come on just another step." He's guiding me on to the platform.

So, I do what he says. I take a few deep breaths – I look at the view. And I try and distance myself from what's really happening. Then suddenly, the operator is doing the countdown "Five … four … three … two … one … BUNGY!" I still don't know why or how, but I JUMPED!

Oh boy! e)<u>What a feeling!</u> Everything in slow motion – you feel like … out of this world! And you're falling, falling, falling and the water's coming closer and closer … AND all of a sudden you come to the end of the rope and you get pulled right back up again and you feel like you're flying. Really! You feel like a bird, then you go down again and up again until finally another guy comes along in a raft and you're lowered into that.

Straight afterwards, I couldn't stop laughing. I felt like an idiot, but I just couldn't stop laughing. I guess after all the tension and fear I just needed to let it all out! I went back to the office and bought the DVD, so I can bore you all with that when I get home.

My time on this computer is running out, so I'd better say goodbye. We're off to Wanaka tomorrow. This is a great trip – NZ is so beautiful – I'm having a fantastic time.

That's all from me for now. All the best to everyone. See ya! :)

Jamie

---

a) Read Jamie's email to his friends. Which phrase best describes his holiday?

1 a working holiday
2 a boring holiday
3 an adventure holiday

b) Who do you think Jamie is writing to?

1 his grandparents, who he is very fond of
2 his friends of the same age
3 lecturers at the university he has just graduated from

c) Which pattern of feeling best describes Jamie's experience?

1 afraid → resigned → relaxed
2 confident → afraid → relaxed
3 confident → afraid → exhilarated

Reading and Writing Portfolio 8

2 Jamie's friend, Tamzen, emails her parents about the news. Fill each gap with one word.

> Had an email from Jamie the other day. He's having a great a) _holiday_ in b) _____
> c) _____ . He's got as far as
> d) _____ , where he did his first ever
> e) _____ f) _____ . He said it
> was incredible, but just before he
> g) _____ , he felt h) _____ ,
> poor thing! The bungy operator had to
> i) _____ him on to the j) _____
> and told him to k) _____ deeply. I can
> just imagine it. In the end, Jamie jumped and he
> said the experience of l) _____ was
> like the whole world was in m) _____
> n) _____ . But when the rope
> o) _____ him up, he felt as though he
> was p) _____ . Sounds scary to me!
> Don't think I'll ever try it myself ...

3 Match these colloquial words/phrases from Jamie's email to definitions 1–6.

awesome	cool	full-on
sweet	freak out	stuff

1 extremely good _awesome_
2 things _____
3 become extremely emotional _____
4 very busy, demanding, intense _____
5 well, fine _____
6 excellent, very good _____

Help with Writing   Informal language

a) Read a)–e), which describe words and expressions associated with informal language. Match them to words/phrases 1–5 in **bold** in Jamie's email.

a) a colloquial word is used ___4___

b) an unnecessary word is added at the beginning of a phrase – similar to a conversation _____

c) words are repeated – similar to a conversation _____

d) a conversational greeting is used _____

e) a noun which has an imprecise meaning is used _____

b) Read 1–5, which describe grammatical features and punctuation associated with informal language. Match them to <u>underlined</u> words/phrases a)–e) in Jamie's email.

1 words are missed out _a)_

2 present verb forms are used to talk about a past event _____

3 a conjunction is used at the beginning of a sentence _____

4 an exclamation that doesn't contain a verb is used _____

5 unconventional punctuation is used for emphasis _____

5 Look again at Tamzen's email in **2**. Choose the best answer.

It has a neutral style ...

a) because Tamzen hasn't seen her parents for a long time and doesn't want to upset them with too much slang.

b) because they are older and don't always use the same informal language.

6 Fill in the gaps with the correct form of words from **3**.

1 Going white-water rafting was the most amazing experience – it was _awesome_ !

2 I had no trouble finding somewhere to stay. It was _____ .

3 I went for this really _____ cycling trip. We hardly had any rest.

4 When I got back to the hostel, I found someone had been through my _____ looking for money.

5 When they left me alone in the forest, I _____ . I felt totally lost.

6 I met some really _____ people. They were really friendly.

7 Look again at Jamie's email. Find informal words/phrases that have the same meaning as a)–j).

a) I will see you later. _See ya!_

b) Until then, everything was all right.
_____

c) … the waiver forms and other documentation of that nature …
_____

d) It was a depth of 43 metres …
_____

e) I still don't know why or how, but I jumped. _____

f) Everything happened in slow motion …
_____

g) It's not good, it's not all right.
_____

h) However, it was very frightening.
_____

i) … the water was coming closer and closer … _____

j) At the same time, I was thinking …
_____

8 Replace the words/phrases in **bold** in this email with these words/phrases to make it more informal.

> ~~Hi there everyone~~   awesome   freaked out   SO AMAZING
> coolest   there's this huge, dark shape that's passing by   But
> Well   full-on   What a thrill!   stuff like that

Hi there everyone
[1]~~Dear All~~,
This is the [2]**best** holiday – every day is [3]**busy** and there's so much to do. [4]**What a thrilling time I'm having!** [5]**To give more detail**, yesterday I went snorkelling on Great Barrier Reef and it was [6]**so extraordinary**. [7]**However**, I [8]**got very worried** when I saw this huge stingray swimming nearby. I was swimming along and [9]**looking at the reef** then all of a sudden, [10]**there was a huge, dark shape that was passing by**. They're incredible creatures – slow and graceful, but a bit menacing. It was [11]**incredible**!

9 **a)** Think of an interesting or exciting event that happened to you. If you can't think of something, you can invent it. Make notes in the table.

who you are writing to	
where you were and what you were doing	
who was there	
any conversation	
how you felt before, during and after	
any specific outcome or result	

b) Write your email and explain what happened.

- Use your notes in **9a)**.
- Use an appropriate level of formality.
- Read and check for mistakes.
- Give your email to your teacher next class.

> Tick the things you can do in English in the Reading and Writing Progress Portfolio, p88.

Guidelines and instructions

Reading information on using a travel card
Writing connecting words in guidelines/instructions; questions as headings
Review conditionals; travel

 Read the guidelines on pages 78 and 79 quickly. Fill in gapped headings 1–6 with questions a)–f).

a) ~~What is an Oyster card?~~
b) How do I top up?
c) What do I do now?
d) Why should I have one?
e) How do I pay for my journey with Oyster?
f) How can I protect my money?

1 *What is an Oyster card?*

Oyster is the cheapest way to pay for single journeys on the bus, Tube and tram in London, DLR and London Overground. You can store cash on your card, check your balance as well as buy and renew tickets or top up cash. You can also protect your money and even manage your Oyster card online. a)In order that you get the most out of your Oyster card, read this guide carefully.

2 _____

b)Besides being faster and easier, it's cheaper!
- Faster: Oyster saves you time – no more queuing for tickets as you can pay in advance.
- Easier: Your Oyster card is reusable – just top it up with cash or renew your Travelcard/Bus Pass when needed.
- Cheaper: Oyster single fares are always cheaper than cash – see examples below.

	Cash single fare	Oyster single fare
Tube (Zone 1)	£4.00	£1.50
Tube (Zones 1–2) (Monday–Friday 7 a.m.–7 p.m.) (All other times including public holidays)	£4.00	£2.00 £1.50
Bus/Tram	£2.00	£0.90

3 _____

You can store cash on your card to pay for single journeys as you go. If you pay as you go, the system will look at your journeys in a 24-hour period* and the amount you pay will be capped. c)Therefore it will always cost you less than the price of an equivalent Day Travelcard or One Day Bus Pass. Our aim is to ensure that Oyster always charges the lowest fare. Where it doesn't, we will refund the difference. If you don't travel much, don't worry – your cash doesn't expire**.

How do I use Oyster?

Touch in and out:
- To ensure you pay the correct fare, when travelling by Tube you must always touch in on the yellow reader at the start of your journey and touch out at the end of your journey. d)Otherwise, you will pay the maximum cash fare.
- When using a bus or tram, you must touch in at the start of your journey, but not at the end.
- Please check for the green light when you touch in or out to ensure your Oyster card has been validated.
- Failure to touch in and/or touch out correctly may result in a Penalty Fare, or you being prosecuted.

4 _____

You can top up your cash balance:
- online at tfl.gov.uk/oyster;
- at Tube station touchscreen ticket machines and ticket offices;
- at some National Rail ticket offices;
- by phone on 0845 330 9876.

*24-hour period is from 4.30 a.m. and before 4.30 a.m. the next day.
**If your card is not used for two years, you will have to reactivate it or claim your unused cash back.

Read the guidelines again and choose the best answer for each question.

1 You can use the Oyster card …
   a) in all major cities in the UK.
   b) on buses all over the UK.
   c) on Tube trains, trams and buses in London.

2 With an Oyster card …
   a) public transport is a little cheaper.
   b) you don't have to buy a ticket before travelling.
   c) you will usually save money compared to paying by cash.

3 Oyster cards …
   a) never expire.
   b) expire after two years.
   c) cannot be used when the balance is below £5.

4 The maximum amount you can put on your card at one time is …
   a) £40.
   b) unlimited.
   c) not stated.

5 If you register your card, …
   a) you do not need to remember its number.
   b) the money on your card is safe if you lose it.
   c) you will get further discounts on journeys you make regularly.

6 You can order an Oyster card …
   a) on the Internet.
   b) over the phone.
   c) at Tube stations.
   d) all of the above.

Auto top-up

With Auto top-up, your Oyster card pay as you go balance can be topped up automatically with either £20 or £40, whenever your balance drops below £5. To set up this service or to get more details visit our website.

5 _____

[e)]As soon as you register your Oyster card, your cash to pay as you go is protected if the card is lost or stolen. You also receive emails from us with information that is important or necessary for you to know, such as details of planned disruptions to your regular journey or new services available on Oyster.
The easiest time to register your Oyster card is when you first get it. It is, however, possible to register your card at a later date:
● at Tube station ticket offices;
● at Oyster Ticket Stops.

6 _____

Now you know why you should have an Oyster card and how to use it, here is how to get one:

1 Apply for your card online at tfl.gov.uk/oyster, at Tube station ticket offices or by phone on 0845 330 9876.
2 Register your card to protect it. You must keep a record of your card number (on the back of the card) and password.

[f)]Frankly, it's as simple as that.

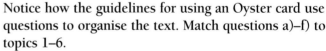
Help with Writing Connecting words in guides/instructions; questions as headings

 a) Match underlined connecting words a)–f) from the guide to their functions 1–6.

1 addition _b)_   4 condition _____
2 time _____   5 comment adverbial _____
3 purpose _____   6 reason and result _____

b) Match functions 1–6 in 3a) to connecting words a)–g).

a) *prior to* _time_
b) *as a result* _____
c) *not only … but …* _____
d) *provided* _____
e) *from then on* _____
f) *so that* _____
g) *in fact* _____

4 **Notice how the guidelines for using an Oyster card use questions to organise the text. Match questions a)–f) to topics 1–6.**

a) How many songs can I put on my MusicBox?
b) What food should I avoid buying?
c) Should I set my alarm at night?
d) How can I use the DVD/CD-ROM drive?
e) How much can I borrow?
f) Should I stay in my vehicle?

1 Home security _____
2 In the event of a breakdown _____
3 Applying for a mortgage _____
4 Using a laptop _____
5 Using an MP3 player _____
6 Eating ethically _____

Reading and Writing Portfolio 9

 5 **a)** Write questions about the Oyster card using the prompts.

1 Why / Oyster card / introduce?

Why was the Oyster card introduced?

> a)**Before Oyster cards were introduced**, most people paid for their journeys on public transport using cash. This resulted in unnecessary delays on buses and at Tube stations.
> b)**Oyster cards have resulted in the transport network becoming virtually cashless**, with over 80% of journeys made in 2008 paid for by Oyster cards.

2 Why / Oyster cards / such / good idea?

....

> c)**It is more convenient and you will save money too.**

3 What / do / if / lose / card?

....

> d)**If** you have registered your card, you can contact us and we'll send you a refund.

4 When / get / card / what / do / first?

....

> Register your card immediately. e)**Then** the money on your card will be protected.

5 What / most important thing / remember / Oyster cards?

....

> Always touch your card on the yellow reader when you enter or leave the station, even if the gate is open, f)**for the reason that then** we know when your journey started and ended.

6 Do / have to / from UK / buy / card?

....

> You do not need to be a UK resident to buy an Oyster card. g)**The truth is that** anyone can buy one from any Tube station.

b) Rewrite a)–g) in **bold** in **5a)** using words/phrases in the box.

Prior to	so that	In fact	From then on
Provided	As a result	Not only ... but ...	

a) *Prior to the introduction of Oyster cards*

b) ....

c) ....

d) ....

e) ....

f) ....

g) ....

6 **a)** Read questions a)–h). Match them to topics 1–4.

a) How do I work out what I spend monthly?
b) What does it do?
c) What is a price-comparison website?
d) How much should I pay into a pension?
e) Where can I use it?
f) Where do I find discount vouchers?
g) Which debts should I pay off first?
h) How can I save if I'm always in debt?

1 Personal finance – how to budget *a)* , *h)*

2 Securing your financial future .... , ...

3 Using a new cashless smartcard .... , ...

4 Saving money – buying things online .... , ...

b) Write guidelines using one of the topics in **6a)**. Use the two questions in **6a)** and your own ideas.

- Think about what to include in an introduction.
- Organise your guidelines using questions in a logical order.
- Use connecting words from **3a)** and **b)**.
- Read and check for mistakes.
- Give your guidelines to your teacher next class.

> Tick the things you can do in English in the Reading and Writing Progress Portfolio, p88.

An extract from a novel

Reading a description of a scene
Writing descriptive language in narratives
Review descriptive verbs

 Read the excerpt quickly. The writer describes several things, people and events. Put them in the order they occur.

a) The people in the restaurant __3__

b) The restaurant _____

c) The person outside the restaurant _____

d) The actions of a person outside the restaurant _____

e) The truck _____

The Grapes of Wrath

First published in 1939, *The Grapes of Wrath* was written by John Steinbeck. It is set in the state of Oklahoma, USA, during the Great Depression, a period of worldwide economic decline which started in 1929. It tells the tale of a family whose farm has been repossessed by the bank and who have decided to walk to the state of California to find work.

In 1940, the novel won the Pulitzer Prize and is considered a classic of American literature.

A huge red transport truck stood in front of the little roadside restaurant. The vertical exhaust pipe muttered softly, and an almost invisible haze of steel-blue smoke hovered over its end. It was a new truck, shining red, and in twelve-inch letters on its sides – OKLAHOMA CITY TRANSPORT COMPANY. Its double tires were new, and a brass padlock stood straight out from the hasp* on the big back doors. Inside the screened restaurant a radio played, quiet dance music turned low the way it is when no one is listening. A small outlet fan turned silently in its circular hole over the entrance, and flies buzzed excitedly about the doors and windows, butting the screens. Inside, one man, the truck driver, sat on a stool and rested his elbows on the counter and looked over his coffee at the lean and lonely waitress. He talked the smart listless language of the roadsides to her. "I seen him about three months ago. He had a operation. Cut somepin out. I forget what." And she – "Doesn't seem no longer than a week I seen him myself. Looked fine then. He's a nice sort

of a guy when he ain't stinko." Now and then the flies roared softly at the screen door. The coffee machine spurted steam, and the waitress, without looking, reached behind her and shut it off.

Outside, a man walking along the edge of the highway crossed over and approached the truck. He walked slowly to the front of it, put his hand on the shiny fender, and looked at the No Riders sticker on the windshield. For a moment he was about to walk on down the road, but instead he sat on the running board on the side away from the restaurant. He was not over thirty. His eyes were very dark brown and there was a hint of brown pigment in his eyeballs. His cheek bones were high and wide, and strong deep lines cut down his cheeks, in curves beside his mouth. His upper lip was long, and since his teeth protruded, the lips stretched to cover them, for this man kept his lips closed. His hands were hard, with broad fingers and nails as thick and ridged as little clam shells. The space between thumb and forefinger and the hams of his hands were shiny with callus**.

*hasp = an old-fashioned word for clasp or piece of metal that fastens two things
**callus = an area of hard thickened skin, especially on the feet or hands

2 Read the extract again and use the context to match these words to definitions a)–i).

haze	hover	fan	lean	listless
screen door	windshield	protruded	broad	

a) stuck out _____

b) very wide _____

c) thin _____

d) a door with fine wire netting, which allows air but not insects to move through _____

e) air that isn't clear because of something such as heat or smoke _____

f) stay in one place in the air _____

g) lacking energy and enthusiasm _____

h) a device used to move the air around _____

i) American English for *windscreen* – the window at the front of a vehicle _____

3 Answer these questions.

1 What does the restaurant description tell you about it?

_____

2 Do you think the man in the restaurant will be there for a long time? Why?/Why not?

_____

3 How do you think the waitress feels about her job? Why?

_____

_____

4 What do you think *stinko* means?

_____

5 The author makes deliberate mistakes in the direct speech to represent the way people speak. <u>Underline</u> the mistakes and rewrite them in standard English.

_____

_____

_____

6 What do you think the 'No Riders' sticker means?

_____

7 Why do you think the man outside the restaurant considers walking on when he sees the sticker?

_____

8 What does the description of the man outside the restaurant tell you about him?

_____

4 The writer uses a range of techniques to make the description as interesting and involving as possible.

- adjectives: *A **huge red** transport truck …*
- adverbs: *The vertical exhaust pipe muttered **softly** …*
- personification: *… exhaust pipe **muttered** …*
- expressive verbs: *… smoke **hovered** over its end.*
- naturalistic language in direct speech: *I **seen** him about three months ago.*
- unusual collocation: *… flies **roared softly** …*
- simile: *His hands were hard, with broad fingers and nails **as thick and ridged as** little clam shells.*

5 a) Find adjectives in the excerpt which describe these things.

1 smoke from the exhaust pipe *steel-blue*

2 the colour of the truck _____

3 the waitress

_____ , _____

4 the restaurant

_____ , _____

5 the music on the radio _____

6 the man's eyes _____

7 the man's cheek bones

_____ , _____

8 the man's fingers _____

b) Find adverbs in the extract which describe how these move.

1 the flies _____

2 the fan _____

3 the man outside _____

c) Find dramatic verbs which describe these things.

1 the movement of the flies

_____ , _____

2 the coffee machine _____

Replace the underlined verbs with the correct form of these dramatic verbs. Use a monolingual dictionary if necessary.

| peer | roar | blaze | weep | rocket |

1 "Stop!" he <u>shouted</u>.

2 The children were <u>running</u> around the room.

3 The sun <u>shone</u> down on them.

4 Everywhere people were <u>crying</u> with happiness.

5 A face was <u>looking</u> through the window.

 Complete these similes.

| ~~stars~~ | a small child | a sheet |
| pigs | a baby's | a rock | ice |

1 His eyes were as <u>bright</u> as   *stars.*

2 They were <u>eating</u> like ....

3 He was <u>crying</u> like ....

4 The bed was as <u>hard</u> as ....

5 Her skin was as <u>soft</u> as ....

6 His face was as <u>white</u> as ....

7 The room was as <u>cold</u> as ....

 Rewrite these sentences to make them more interesting and engaging. Use techniques from 4.

1 There was a loud noise as the door opened and the woman walked into the room. She was tall and had nice clothes. Her face was cold.

....

....

....

2 A man stood in front of the house. He was smoking. Every so often he would look up at the window of the house.

....

....

....

3 "Are you going to tell her?" she asked him. "I might do," he said. "It depends."

....

....

....

4 The doorbell rang. He stood up, walked to the door and he opened it. A boy was standing in front of him.

....

....

....

 a) Imagine you are writing a description of a scene for a creative writing competition in a student magazine. Make notes in the table.

Paragraph 1: Set the scene • What are you describing? • What effect do you want to have on the reader?	
Paragraph 2: Explain the sights, sounds, smells • Where is it? • What can you sense/feel?	
Paragraph 3: Describe a person or people • Start with an overall impression • Focus on details	
Paragraph 4: Describe something that happened • What did the person/people say or do?	

b) Write your description.

● Use your notes in **9a)**.
● Use a wide range of vocabulary to describe movement, light/colour and sounds in the scene.
● Read and check for mistakes.
● Give your description to your teacher next class.

> Tick the things you can do in English in the Reading and Writing Progress Portfolio, p88.

Accurate Writing

Connecting words: addition `AW1.1`

1   Fill in the gaps with these connecting words/phrases. Sometimes there is more than one possible answer.

> as well   too   also   not only
> what's more   besides

1   His grumbling is .... boring, but it's also disruptive.

2   We get on well and we've got a lot in common, ...

3   I love gossip, but I'm .... aware that it can be dangerous.

4   I overheard Martin talking about the rumour, ...

5   I've already apologised for the mistake. .... , I didn't do it on purpose, as you know.

6   You're out of your depth. .... your temper is out of control.

Spelling: homophones `AW1.2`

2   Find an incorrect spelling of a homophone in each sentence. Correct the mistakes.

1   I don't know if there at home at the moment.

2   Whose coming to your party tomorrow?

3   We really would have helped you if we could of.

4   You're going to be late for you're meeting if you don't leave soon.

5   I would have been here earlier but they're weren't any trains.

6   I think that's their car but I don't know who's bike that is.

Connecting words: time (1) `AW2.1`

3   Choose the correct connecting word/phrase. Sometimes there is more than one possible answer.

[1]*Ever since/From then on/As* Aileen and Adam's son Louis drew his first picture, they've suspected him of being artistically gifted. Just before his fifth birthday, they became convinced.

[2]*While/Meanwhile/As* Adam was running Louis's bath one evening, Louis showed him a picture he had drawn. Adam [3]*afterwards/first/originally* thought it was just a typical toddler's drawing and being busy, he barely looked at it. However, [4]*the moment/then/ as soon as* Louis was in bed, he started tidying the bathroom and spotted his son's picture again. Adam was astounded – the picture was simple, but clearly recognisable as Louis.

[5]*Ever since/From then on/ Meanwhile*, Aileen and Adam have done everything they can to support their child's talent. At weekends, Louis attended special classes for artistic children. Now, five years later and aged ten, Louis is holding his first exhibition.

[6]*Meanwhile/Afterwards/While* some of London's art collectors have started to take note of the young talent. One of the paintings at his exhibition was bought for £15,000!

Punctuation: apostrophes `AW2.2`

4   Correct the mistakes in these sentences.

1   Its highly unlikely well be there on time.

2   Someone left this coat at my sons party. Is it your's?

3   We aren't exactly sure of it's age but my husbands' friend thinks its about 200 years old.

4   My parents' are in their 70s but theyre very active.

5   The towns unspoilt character makes it a lovely place to visit.

6   That ones mine, your one's are still in the fridge.

Connecting words: contrast (1) AW3.1

5 Fill in the gaps with these connecting words/phrases. Sometimes there is more than one possible answer.

> even though   however   whereas   but   although

1 I'm a determined person. _____ , I'm also a good listener.

2 Gail's sister is very confident _____ Gail is quite a cautious person.

3 I got over the flu weeks ago, _____ I'm still feeling under the weather.

4 _____ our car's getting on a bit, it still runs as smoothly as the day it was bought.

5 It's still a bit on the chilly side in here _____ the heating is on full.

Spelling: one word, two words or hyphenated AW3.2

6 Choose the correct spelling.

1 I *may be/maybe* thrifty but I'm never tight-fisted.
2 Coughs and colds are part of *every day/everyday* life for a toddler.
3 He's only 15, but he's already almost *two metres/two-metres* tall!
4 I don't think *any one/anyone* would say you're timid!
5 You've insulted *every one/everyone* of my ideas!
6 Is there *any way/anyway* you could get here before five o'clock?

Connecting words: contrast (2) AW4.1

7 Join sentence beginnings 1–5 to sentence endings a)–e) using these connecting words.

> ~~despite~~   nonetheless,   However,   Nevertheless,   although

1 They're running the story *despite*   *b)*
2 He doesn't read any newspapers, but _____
3 The story didn't make the broadsheets. _____
4 The stories emerged during a very busy news period. _____
5 The star has remained silent until now _____

a) seems to be well informed about current events.
b) ~~the actor threatening to sue for libel.~~
c) they received a lot of coverage.
d) his agent issued a short press release.
e) it was all over the tabloids.

Punctuation: capital letters and full stops AW4.2

8 Rewrite this paragraph, adding capital letters and full stops.

newspapers in the uk are commonly split into broadsheets and tabloids the most popular broadsheet, which is published monday to friday, is the *daily telegraph* it's owned by brothers david and frederick barclay, who live on the tiny island of brecqhou in the english channel the most popular daily tabloid is the *sun* and is owned by rupert murdoch, the australian media mogul, who also owns *the times* and the tv station sky

Newspapers in the UK _____

_____

_____

_____

Connecting words: time (2) AW5.1

9 Rewrite these sentences using the connecting words/phrases in brackets.

1 I did a nine-to-five job in an office and then last year I became self-employed. (previously)

   Last year I became self-employed. Previously I did a nine-to-five job in an office.

2 We are seeing a lot of each other at the moment. (lately)

3 I was earning a pittance and then I joined this company. (prior to)

4 We would like to make a formal offer of employment. It follows our conversation yesterday. (subsequent)

5 I've been working for a month but before that I was unemployed. (up until)

Accurate Writing

 10 Correct the mistakes in **bold** in these sentences.

1 She told me the news **straight away**.

2 **Of lately**, she's been really fed up with work.

3 She'd **final** decided it was time to move on.

4 I knew she **instantly** was making a mistake.

5 And before **give in** her resignation, I pleaded with her to listen to me.

6 **Later an hour**, I had convinced her to think a little harder.

7 And **in the end of the day**, over coffee, she agreed to think on her decision for another week.

Spelling: *ie* or *ei* AW5.2

 11 **a)** Complete these words with *ie* or *ei*.

1 sc____nce   6 conc____ted

2 suffic____nt   7 shr____k

3 ____ther   8 p____ce

4 ach____ve   9 c____ling

5 n____ghbour   10 for____gn

b) Which words in **11a)** have the pronunciation /iː/?

_____, _____, _____

_____, _____, _____

Connecting words: purpose AW6.1

 12 Rewrite 1–5 using the words/phrases in brackets.

1 I left a message because I didn't want her to worry. (so that)

I left a message so that she wouldn't be worried.

2 She got dressed in the dark because she didn't want to disturb her sister. (so as)

_____

3 We worked late to avoid working at the weekend. (in order that)

_____

4 Please provide us with a daytime telephone number. Then we can contact you quickly. (in order for)

_____

5 They spoke quietly because they didn't want anyone to overhear them. (so)

_____

Punctuation: colons and semi-colons AW6.2

 13 Look at these pairs of sentences. In which sentence can you use a colon (:) or semi-colon (;) at the position marked with * ?

1a) I used to live in Italy* I love its beautiful cities and amazing food. _semi-colon_

b) Italy is a wonderful country* the cities are beautiful and the food is amazing. _colon_

2a) She doesn't eat meat* she's a vegetarian for health reasons. _____

b) He's vegan* he used to be vegetarian. _____

3a) Stocks and shares are at an all-time low* this is despite low interest rates. _____

b) The financial markets are very unstable at present* investors lack confidence. _____

4a) I recently started learning the piano* I have no musical talent. _____

b) I've taken up drumming* I've always wanted to play them. _____

5a) We've got two options* break now for ten minutes or carry on and finish early. _____

b) There were three alternatives* going by train was what we agreed on. _____

Connecting words: condition AW7.1

 14 Choose the correct connecting word/phrase. Sometimes both answers are correct.

1 A *Supposing/Otherwise* he mentions the problem today, what will you say?

B *As long as/Imagine* he doesn't get at me, I'll do my best to help.

2 A I don't know *whether/if* he's guilty or not.

B He must be, *unless/otherwise* he wouldn't have tried to run off from the police.

3 A *Provided/Imagine* being able to retire early, what would you do?

B I'm not sure. However, *if/unless* you had lots of hobbies, you'd get bored very quickly!

4 A *If/Whether* you can get round to it today, I'd be extremely grateful.

B *Assuming/Provided* nothing unexpected arises, I'm certain I can.

Punctuation: commas AW7.2

 15 Add between one and three commas to each sentence.

1 Despite the enormous outcry plans for the new airport are proceeding.
2 Incredibly they got away with the robbery.
3 "I can't get through to him" she said desperately.
4 I travelled to Italy Spain France and Turkey last year.
5 My eldest brother who lives abroad is a rich successful businessman.
6 The wallpaper which was a disgusting mix of brown yellow and green was peeling off the walls.
7 The address is 120 Hills Road Newtown Hampshire.

Comment adverbials AW8.1

 16 Replace the <u>underlined</u> phrases with a comment adverbial in the box. Sometimes there is more than one possible answer.

> Apparently,   Fortunately,   Quite honestly,   Surely
> Frankly,   Amazingly,   According to   Obviously,

1 <u>Being truthful with you</u>, I'm just not interested in your excuses.
2 <u>It is evident that</u> Joe won't be able to come.
3 <u>I'm not sure it's true, but</u> I've heard he's resigned.
4 <u>It is because of good luck</u> we weren't hurt.
5 <u>What is extremely surprising is</u> she didn't seem to care.
6 <u>My direct opinion is that</u> you shouldn't have lent him the money.
7 <u>I am surprised that it isn't true</u> you have heard of the Rolling Stones.
8 <u>From what I've heard from</u> Lee, we'll be there in plenty of time.

Spelling: commonly misspelled words AW8.2

 17 Correct the spelling of one word in each sentence.

1 If you run your own business, you should keep all receits.
2 The goverment has succeeded in winning its third election.
3 The effects of the medicine have been exaggerrated.
4 Please acquaint yourself with the rules for student acommodation at the university.
5 The man admited giving the police a false address.
6 If necessary, I can arrange for one of my colleages to attend the meeting.

Connecting words: reason and result AW9.1

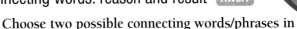 **18** Choose two possible connecting words/phrases in each sentence.

1 *Due/Owing/As a result* to the technology advancing so rapidly, solar panels are becoming increasingly popular on houses.
2 *Since/Due to/As a result of* economic decline, record levels of business are closing.
3 *Because of/Owing to/As a result* demand, property has always been expensive in the capital.
4 *As/Since/Consequently* interest rates are so low, the housing market is expected to show signs of recovery soon.
5 The total amount of aid this year is similar to the figure for last year – *consequently/as a result of/therefore* in real terms it has shrunk.
6 *Because of/As a result/Due to* rising factory costs, the company reported a drop in profits this year.

Spelling: *-ible* or *-able* AW9.2

 19 a) Complete the table with words ending in *-ible* or *-able*.

> ~~aud-~~   vis-   cred-   port-
> valu-   memor-   laugh-   elig-

-ible	-able
audible	

b) Match the words in **19a)** to their meanings a)–h).

a) able to be heard _audible_
b) likely to be remembered ....
c) able to be carried ....
d) having the necessary qualities ....
e) able to be seen ....
f) foolish and not deserving serious consideration ....
g) worth a lot of money ....
h) able to be believed ....

Advanced Reading and Writing Progress Portfolio

Tick the things you can do in English.

Portfolio	Reading	Writing
1 p54	☐ I can understand in detail a complex analysis where viewpoints are discussed.	☐ I can write a clear, well-structured article on a complex subject. ☐ I can develop ideas systematically within paragraphs.
2 p57	☐ I can read complex texts with the use of a dictionary.	☐ I can use a monolingual dictionary to improve and check my writing. ☐ I can write engaging texts which are appropriate for the reader.
3 p60	☐ I can read in detail a complex proposal.	☐ I can use a variety of discourse markers to compare and contrast information. ☐ I can put together information from different sources and relate it in a coherent proposal with recommendations.
4 p63	☐ I can read a complex discussion, understanding in detail the main points of an argument.	☐ I can write about a complex issue, giving my point of view and supporting it with reasons and examples. ☐ I can use a variety of techniques to introduce and structure the main ideas in my argument.
5 p66	☐ I can extract information, ideas and opinions from an article about a personal experience.	☐ I can write an article which describes an experience and my feelings about it. ☐ I can use a variety of techniques to personalise my writing.
6 p69	☐ I can understand in detail letters of complaint.	☐ I can write a detailed formal letter of complaint. ☐ I can write formally correct letters selecting appropriate style and content.
7 p72	☐ I can read a complex review of a literary work.	☐ I can write a review of a book or film. ☐ I can use a variety of cohesive devices to make my writing more interesting, link ideas more effectively and avoid repetition.
8 p75	☐ I can understand in detail an informal letter or email.	☐ I can write informal letters or emails, demonstrating an appropriate style with a wide range of techniques.
9 p78	☐ I can understand long complex instructions.	☐ I can write detailed, and organised instructions. ☐ I can use a wide variety of connecting words in my writing.
10 p81	☐ I can go beyond the concrete plot of a narrative and grasp implicit meanings, ideas and connections.	☐ I can write a detailed description or imaginative text. ☐ I can use a wide variety of vocabulary and descriptive techniques to make my writing interesting and engaging.